Emotional and Beha
A Reader

Edited by
John Visser and Steve Rayner

A QEd Publication

Published in 1999

ISBN 1 898873 10 0

Published by QEd, The Rom Building, Eastern Avenue, Lichfield, Staffordshire WS13 6RN

Further copies of this book may be obtained from:
QEd, The Rom Building, Eastern Avenue, Lichfield, Staffordshire WS13 6RN

Typeset in Times New Roman and printed in the UK by Stowes (Stoke-on-Trent).

Emotional and Behavioural Difficulties
A Reader

Contents

Biographical Notes

Biographical Notes

The Editors

John Visser has taught in mainstream and special schools. He is widely known for his staff development and consultancy in schools in the areas of differentiation, teaching and learning and classroom management. He is currently at the University of Birmingham where he is co-course leader for the EBD professional development courses. John has published a number of articles and books on EBD together with colleagues within the EBD research team. He served nine years on the national executive of AWCEBD as treasurer and was a founder member of NASEN for whom he is President in 1999 - 2000.

Steve Rayner has taught in both mainstream and special education. He has worked for the most part in residential and day provision for pupils with Emotional and Behavioural Difficulties and is now a lecturer in special education at the University of Birmingham. He is currently a course leader for the EBD Programme of Study in the Professional Development Course at the School of Education and has published books and articles in the areas of EBD, the management of special education and educational psychology.

The Contributors

Bernard Allen studied Psychology at Newcastle University and has worked extensively with young people who have emotional and behavioural difficulties. He obtained his first headship in 1989 and since then has successfully led two specialist schools. His has written for numerous publications and is the author of *The Children Act Up*, *Children in Control*, and *Holding Back*.

Bill Gribble is a senior education officer. He has worked in a variety of educational establishments ranging from a secure unit for serious young offenders to day school. As a distance education tutor for the University of Birmingham and a course director for an M.Ed module with the University of Wales: Bangor, he is valued for his insight into the behaviour management of the EBD child.

Paul Howard has over twenty-five years experience in the education service. Formerly a youth and community worker, he taught for nine years in a special school for pupils with EBD and, from that base, pioneered outreach work in mainstream primary schools before going on to lecture in the SEN division of Thames Polytechnic. Paul was the first headteacher of the Behaviour Support Service in the London Borough of Newham and during eleven years in that position was actively engaged in the development and implementation of the LEA's inclusive education policy. Paul now works as a freelance trainer and consultant.

Mark Provis is Head of Training, Advice and Consultancy Services for INCLUDE - a national charity promoting the inclusion of all young people in mainstream education, training and employment. He has taught in mainstream and specialist settings and has managed a large behavioural intervention service. Qualified in Educational and Occupational Psychology, Mark has been a senior manager in local government - as Assistant Director of Education and as Assistant Director of Management Development.

Dave Shaw. After teaching in a variety of mainstream and special schools, Dave moved into social service provision in Manchester, where he now works as an advocacy, support and advisory teacher for the city's social services department. In this role he has been able to originate and develop a range of strategies designed to support looked-after children and young people in their education.

Richard Stakes has taught children with special educational needs in mainstream schools for over twenty-five years. Currently, he works on professional development courses for teachers of children with SEN. He has a research fellowship at Sheffield Hallam University, where he is investigating strategies used by classroom teachers in mainstream schools with children with autism.

Chris Travell has experience of teaching in a number of special schools and was deputy headteacher of a school catering for pupils with severe learning difficulties for five years. He then undertook training at Birmingham University in Educational Psychology and now works as an Educational Psychologist for Worcestershire County Council. Chris has also been a Regional Tutor on the Birmingham University EBD Distance Education Course since its inception in 1993. He has a wide variety of interests alongside the field of EBD, including systemic approaches to intervention, the application of personal construct psychology, the importance of listening to children and the promotion of inclusive education.

Chapter One

Emotional and Behavioural Difficulties: perspectives on perspectives

by Chris Travell

Why is the number of pupils excluded from UK schools rising year on year? Why are proportionately more boys than girls excluded from school? Why are proportionately more African-Caribbean boys excluded from school than any other group? Why are more and more children being prescribed psycho-stimulant drugs to control their behaviour?

A simple answer to these questions might be that there is an increasing number of children with emotional and behavioural difficulties (EBD), for reasons which range from growing numbers of marriage breakdowns, increasing social and economic divisions within society, falling standards in schools, a lack of parental discipline or rising levels of pollution. But what are these 'emotional and behavioural difficulties' to which we can glibly refer? Are they real, and, if so, how can we understand them?

Within the field of education the concept of 'emotional and behavioural difficulties' may at first appear straightforward. The term implies there is a homogenous group of children, a subgroup of the population of children with 'special educational needs', whose needs can be assessed and met with special educational provision (for example, in EBD special schools). In Circular 9/94 (DfE, 1994) the Department for Education described these children in the following terms:

> '...emotional and behavioural difficulties lie on the continuum between behaviour which challenges teachers but is within normal, albeit unacceptable, bounds and that which is indicative of serious mental illness. The distinction between normal but stressed behaviour, emotional and behavioural difficulties, and behaviour arising from mental illness is important because each needs to be treated differently.'
>
> (DfE, 1994, p7, para 2)

By its very nature the term 'emotional and behavioural difficulties' implies children with this label have problems which need to be solved. Travell (1999) examines various theoretical perspectives on human development, and how these might account for the occurrence of emotional and behavioural difficulties in some children. Here, however, the reader is invited to stand back from this traditional approach to conceptualising and intervening with children and examine the philosophical, social and political issues which might contribute to the understanding of child development and EBD.

It is important to recognise that an analysis of research and the formulation of theories concerning child development must take into account the perspectives of the researchers themselves, and of their prevailing social and political climates. Cultural considerations, accepted philosophies and moral attitudes towards children, and the nature of education systems themselves, will also influence research. Although researchers may be ethically sound, their areas of study are also likely to be determined by who funds their research. Thus, for example, more research is likely to be conducted into trialling drugs to control behaviour, funded by rich drug companies, than into sociological interventions, for which limited funds may be available and conclusions more difficult to establish. Similarly, Government-funded educational research is more likely to focus on the examination of 'best practice' within the current system, than to investigate innovative concepts and understandings, experimental designs, new systems or untested methods and approaches.

In order to focus these issues more closely, some of the significant dichotomies which are relevant in the area of child development as it impinges on the construct of EBD will be examined. It is recommended that the reader considers these dichotomies in some detail and applies the issues they raise to the various theoretical perspectives examined in Travell (1999). This will assist the reader to choose which perspectives might particularly help them when developing intervention strategies for the pupils with whom they work.

Nature or nurture?
One of the key aspects to consider when looking at emotional and behavioural development is that regarding the relative contributions of heredity and the environment (the nature-nurture debate). Most researchers agree that both have a part to play, but different theorists

8

stress the relative importance of one or the other in relation to different areas of development or difficulty. In addition, philosophical and political viewpoints have an impact on thinking in this area.

Although very few individuals hold viewpoints in the debate as extreme as those referred to below, and therefore the debate itself is now less real, it is important to recognise from where popular views originate and to where they can lead. As the reader examines various theoretical approaches to understanding EBD, it is advisable to give some thought to their underlying philosophies, and the degree to which they present a pessimistic or optimistic outlook for pupils with EBD.

Those who stress the contribution of heredity, present an essentially fatalistic view of EBD, locating problems as internal to the child. Personal responsibility is stressed and the role of society is to categorise and control those who are born with defective genes. Society, primarily influenced by those with medical qualifications, dictates what is 'normal', and individuals must conform to this norm. Those considered abnormal must receive suitable treatment. In its extreme form such thinking leads to eugenics, aimed at eliminating problem individuals and 'perfecting' the human race. Minority groups are particularly at risk from this approach.

The nature side of the nature-nurture debate focuses specifically on the contribution of genetic make-up to development. If indeed it were possible to identify the gene which predisposes individuals to have EBD, then geneticists would seek ways to modify the chromosomes of future individuals so as to eliminate the gene and thus the EBD. For certain medical conditions and syndromes (e.g. Down's syndrome) links have already been established and genetic counselling is regularly given. Furthermore, for some conditions (e.g. cystic fibrosis) gene therapy techniques have been developed whereby the genetic information of a living individual can be modified in order to alleviate the condition. However, linking genetic information to difficulties which are socially constructed and defined, such as EBD (or even criminality), is a step of a different order. This would lead to social engineering of an unprecedented nature, and could have immense repercussions for the future of the human race.

Researchers and theorists who see the contribution of the environment as most important present a more optimistic view, seeing EBD (to the extent that this is accepted as a concept) as resulting from unhealthy relationships and/or social conditions. Stress is placed on the responsibility of others to assist children to change, and individuals are valued in their own right. There is, therefore, no concept of what is 'normal' as each individual's development is the natural product of the environment in which they are reared. Solutions to problems are jointly negotiated between all interested parties, rather than imposed with a view to achieving a norm. In its extreme form this approach can deny all personal responsibility, dispense with social rules and ultimately lead to anarchy.

Within-child or without-child?

A relative of the nature-nurture debate is the within-child without-child dichotomy. This again has to do with where the problem of EBD is located, and where intervention should be focused.

A within-child perspective sees EBD as stemming from the children themselves. This would include genetic explanations, but also explanations resulting from, for example, other biological or psychodynamic perspectives. Especially from a psychodynamic perspective a strong link is made between emotions and behaviour, behavioural difficulties being seen to stem from a failure to resolve internal conflicts. Where children display EBD, which would normally be identified by the child meeting certain adult-devised criteria, for example as specified in DSM-1V (APA, 1994), the solution would be seen in terms of treatment (e.g. drugs or psychotherapy) for the child.

A without-child perspective, in manner similar to the 'nurture' side of the nature-nurture debate, focuses on environmental factors which might contribute to EBD. This perspective does not start by assuming that because there is a problem, the problem is with the child. It is open to examining other possible explanations, such as that the adults in the child's life are behaving inappropriately. Behaviour might be seen as something learned without the involvement of emotions, or could be viewed as an expression of emotion in response to some environmental event. This approach can be threatening to adults, who usually feel they are right, and that they should be in control. It is important, however, for the promotion of healthy child development, and for the progress of a healthy society, that adults should examine their own behaviour and practices towards children as much as they examine the behaviour and responses of children with whom they work.

10

Individual responsibility or collective responsibility?

Closely associated with the issues above is the question of who is responsible for a child's behaviour: who is responsible for the causes of EBD and whose responsibility is it to put things right? To a degree the answer to these questions will vary according to the age of the child, but ultimately are children responsible for their own behaviour, or are schools, parents and the community at large?

The extent to which parents are responsible for the behaviour of their children, especially when pupils may be presenting difficulties in school, is open to debate. How much do schools cause or contribute to difficulties, or how much can parents or the pupils themselves be held to account? Even when it is acknowledged that out-of-school factors are of key influence, does this absolve the school of the responsibility for trying to bring about change? What responsibilities do other agencies, for example, the social services, have in this regard?

Sometimes 'responsibility' is confused with 'blame'. When this happens with respect to EBD there is usually considerable motivation for those with responsibility to place the 'blame' elsewhere. Because of this, 'nature' and 'within-child' explanations hold great attraction for all concerned. If EBD is seen from a medical or mental illness perspective, the cause is no-one's fault; EBD is a medical accident. However, this view can have serious implications for the child, particularly if there is in reality no medical condition which can be proved.

The relationship between cause and responsibility is complex. From a paternalistic, medical perspective, if a child is born with defective genes, or has acquired some illness, it is society's responsibility to offer treatment or cure, if necessary in an EBD school. This often gives the child a clear message that they are at fault, with little understanding of why, or how they can put things right. It is far easier for those in authority to act in this way than to challenge aspects of parenting, schooling or society as a whole, which may in fact be far greater contributors to the existence of EBD.

Even when the responsibilities of adults and society are acknowledged, there comes a point when each individual has to accept responsibility for their own actions and situation. From a legal perspective this is highlighted by the age of criminal responsibility, and currently these issues are being looked at carefully by the Government.

The courts can modify the point at which an individual is held responsible for their actions on the basis of their 'cognitive' ability or when they are considered mentally ill. This gives great power to those with qualifications to 'medically' diagnose. It is interesting to note that Circular 9/94 (DfE, 1994) reflects some of this approach by placing EBD on a continuum between 'sporadic naughtiness' and 'mental illness', without specifying where the cut-off points might be.

 As with the dichotomies referred to above, it is for the reader to reflect on these issues in the light of developmental theories (see for example Travell, 1999). Of central importance is transcending the notion of 'blame' whilst acknowledging where responsibility for change lies. If change is to take place, be effective and long-lasting, it is likely to come about through partnership, participation and an acceptance of shared responsibility, most importantly with the child him/herself.

Inclusion or exclusion?
Perspectives on inclusion and exclusion go well beyond the field of EBD, but have particular relevance to the education of children so-labelled. 'Inclusive education' can describe a situation where all children, irrespective of their differences, are educated together within the same school, even though they may not all be in the same class at the same time. The central point is that the curriculum offered by the school, and the teaching methods used, are suitable for all children. Primarily, children are not expected to adapt to the school system, the school system is expected to adapt to the needs of the children therein. There are no children for whom this task is considered too great, even though extra resources may be required. In such an inclusive education system no child would be excluded from school and no child would be sent to a segregated special school.

In the field of EBD a number of key elements are required for inclusive education to work. These include an essentially 'humanistic' view of children (i.e. that they are inherently good and need unconditional positive regard to thrive), a flexible approach to the curriculum, flexible teaching approaches, highly skilled teachers and adequate resources. Further discussion regarding the essential elements of effective schooling for children with EBD, and how these might lead to greater inclusion, can be found in Cole, Visser and Upton (1998).

There is an important difference between inclusive education and integrated education, the approach to special education of the nineteen-eighties. Integrated education essentially involves pupils with difficulties being sent to mainstream schools, having been taught to, or being expected to, adapt to the systems currently in existence there. The onus is on the pupil to adapt, whilst the system remains the same. Inclusive education, however, involves pupils 'with difficulties' remaining in their local schools, and the school systems adapting to meet their needs.

Fundamental philosophies and practices within schools might need to change for inclusion to be successful. An example of change regarding EBD would be to see it as individual difference which might be explained from a number of different theoretical viewpoints, rather than as something wrong with the child. This does not preclude the view that there are changes the child needs to make, but these would be seen as part of a process which involved changes to be made by others as well. Whatever the viewpoint and whatever the perceived cause, however, the child would be accepted as a member of the community in their own right, with an entitlement to education within and as a part of the community, rather than as someone who should be excluded from it or sent for treatment elsewhere.

The implications of exclusion from school, and for education in segregated provision, in addition to reflecting society's understanding of EBD, also has significant implications for the future of society itself. What will be the future for those who are being excluded from the mainstream of society now by being excluded from mainstream schools? As such individuals get older it may be possible to permanently exclude a proportion of them in prisons or mental institutions, but what of the rest? If we are to move towards a more socially inclusive society, one of the most challenging areas for change is the field of EBD. If our understanding of EBD in children leads to exclusion and segregated provision, the reality of social inclusion will never be achieved.

EBD as a construct

In the opening paragraphs of this chapter 'emotional and behavioural difficulties' was described as a 'construct', and it is this notion of a construct to which we now return. A construct can be seen as part of a belief system, and thus when the label 'EBD' is applied to a child it will have different meanings for different people, including the child him/

herself. The term is also 'socially constructed' - i.e. it has a collective meaning within our society as a whole, as defined, for example, in Circular 9/94 (DfE, 1994). Essentially, EBD has been constructed by adults working within the education system in an attempt to define and intervene with difficulties presented to the system by children who do not fit, or who challenge its rules. This 'social construct' may differ significantly from the construct of the individual, be it parent, teacher or child.

It is important to recognise that whether a child 'has EBD' or not is not a fact, it is a belief. The child becomes officially labelled EBD when there is agreement at an official level, i.e. when there is an acceptance amongst the professionals and parents concerned that the child's behaviour meets socially constructed criteria. Whether a child 'has EBD' or not, therefore, will be a belief of the adults associated with him/her based on their personal constructs and understanding of the socially constructed criteria. However, when the label is attached to a child through official channels (for example on an Individual Education Plan, in a Statement of Special Educational Needs, by a child psychiatrist or by virtue of a child being sent to an EBD school) it assumes great significance for the child. It is also essential to realise that constructs of EBD at an individual or societal level will influence the nature and interpretation of research, from both the point of view of the conductor and student of research.

One of the difficulties with adult constructions of EBD is they rarely take account of the constructions of children themselves. For instance, how often do adults consider the sense a child makes of being labelled as EBD? What impact will this have on their behaviour? A recent article (Wearmouth, 1999) describes how the label 'maladjusted' seriously affected the self-perceptions of an individual and had a consequent negative impact on his future life. In the light of this, what impact does giving a child drugs every day to control their behaviour have on their view of themselves, and how will this affect their capacity for self-control in the future?

It is the author's contention that these factors must be taken into account in any attempt to 'understand' EBD. EBD is not a disease for which the causal bacteria, virus or brain lesion can be identified and medically treated; it is a construct which draws on societal, cultural and individual histories and perspectives. It is of crucial importance for adults to examine their own reasons for determining a child 'has EBD' before deciding whether the child or its environment should change, or whether intervention is appropriate at all.

Each reader will have a different construct of EBD, a different view of its causes and different ideas about intervention. It is not the aim of this chapter to promote one particular perspective. Rather, the aim is to encourage the reader to develop a construct of EBD which is based on a sound knowledge of theories of child development together with examination of their own and society's philosophical and political perspectives on the issue. Developing a construct of EBD in this way should enable the reader to formulate informed intervention strategies which have clear rationales, and which, when challenged, can be shown to be in the best interests of the children with whom they work.

References

American Psychiatric Association (APA) (1994) *Diagnostic and statistical manual of mental disorders* (DSM-1V). Washington, DC: APA.

Cole, T., Visser, J. and Upton, G. (1998) *Effective Schooling for Pupils with Emotional and Behavioural Difficulties.* London: David Fulton Publishers.

Department for Education (DfE) (1994) *The Education of Children with Emotional and Behavioural Difficulties* (Circular 9/94). London: DfE.

Travell, C. (1999) *Approaches to Understanding EBD and its Development* (Unit 1, EDSE06). Birmingham: University of Birmingham.

Wearmouth, J. (1999) 'Another one flew over: "maladjusted" Jack's perception of his label', *British Journal for Special Education* 26 (1), 15-22.

Chapter Two

A Case History of Provision for Pupils with Emotional and Behavioural Difficulties

by Steve Rayner

Introduction

This chapter will use a fictional case study describing one boy's experience of provision for pupils with emotional and behavioural difficulties (EBD). The intention is to use the story of this young person to explore some of the key issues emerging from a history of EBD provision, which arguably are as relevant today as they were yesterday. The idea is not original. It is taken from a poem I was given during my first year of teaching in a residential special school for pupils with EBD. I always thought that the poem was very clever and would one day serve a useful purpose. I hope that by the end of this chapter the reader will agree that this purpose has been realised. The poem, entitled 'The Ballad of a Malad', a title clearly dating it, is included in its original form as an appendix. I am afraid I am unable to acknowledge the source as it was handed to me as an anonymously written piece of work.

The aim of this chapter is to offer the reader a more focused consideration of key themes relating to making provision for a pupil with EBD. These themes inform the making and implementation of provision and include:

- *purpose* - the key themes of punishment, welfare and education;
- *principles* - a synthesis of theory and practice;
- *placement* - matching individual need with professional resource;
- *intervention* - matching stated policy and provision with professional praxis;
- *provision* - questions related to type and pattern of provision and the key issues of inclusion and exclusion;
- *management* - the key themes of control, quality and success.

The question of effective provision for young people and children experiencing EBD begins and ends with the challenge of meeting the educational and personal needs of the individual. It is perhaps true that this fundamental point is too easily lost, as professionals increasingly focus upon and become involved with issues related to resource, management and provision.

The themes previously identified are understood to be central to organising and administering a response to EBD. It is nevertheless worth repeating that individual need always stands at the centre of any provision which is made to support pupils or young people experiencing EBD. It is, furthermore, anticipated that a professional perspective which takes a view on each of these key themes for provision at an individual level will, in turn, at a broader level, begin to perceive the same issues determining the nature of provision developed as part of a wider platform of policy and practice. There is, finally, the notion proposed here that a relationship exists between perceptions of emotional and behavioural difficulties and their definition, such that the making of policy, the shaping of provision and ensuing professional practice are inextricably linked.

The chapter, to sum up, will attempt to give the reader material to discuss and an opportunity to further reflect upon the topic of provision for pupils with EBD. It will also provide a platform for building a wider frame of reference as well as point to related questions of intervention with EBD.

Meet Billy Bovver
For the purpose of this chapter, I first met Billy Bovver in the mid-eighties. He was 16 going on 6, and nearing the end of statutory school age. Ironically, Billy had not been in school for most of his life. He described himself as a 'skinhead' and a party member of the infamous 'Firm'. He was happiest, he declared, living in the shadow of Stamford Bridge and did his best to see every match Chelsea played. This was not always easy, as Billy had been away for most of his life.

Billy clearly followed a particular fashion, with a close-shaved hairstyle, and three ear-studs in his nose. He favoured wearing denim jeans, a checked button-down shirt, and gleaming, brightly polished, brown Doctor Martin boots. He would typically wear his sleeves rolled up, proudly displaying a tattoo on each arm. One was a picture of a well-endowed woman whom he claimed was his mother, the other was the Chelsea football club badge. Billy presented as an articulate but somewhat moody individual. He was full of bravado when you first met him, but after a while would become more serious, and nervous, and take pleasure in being cynical yet appear unhappy.

Billy had lot to say about his life. He was born on the Isle of Wight. His start in life had been tough. His father had been an alcoholic. His mother had always swung between neglecting him and then smothering him with money and affection. He had almost immediately been identified at play school as a difficult child. The staff, he remembered, had had to stop him from playing with the girls in the Wendy house. He had also been referred to the doctor because of hygiene-related problems and to the Child Guidance Clinic because of his inappropriate behaviour.

Billy believed that his mother was a prostitute. He remembered a long line of 'uncles' visiting the house before he went to school. He had not seen her, however, for several years, and could not remember the last time he had seen his father. He remembered his father going to prison for 15 years when he was five or six years old. Something to do with an attempted robbery of a building society. A social worker had taken him to visit once, but when they got there, his father had been in trouble and they could not see him. He had been in care since he was five and was now looked after by the local authority. He had three brothers and two sisters, but again, he could not remember the last time he had seen them or, for that matter, where they were at that time. They were all being looked after by different local authorities.

Billy's educational record was a story of new placements and movement from 'pillar to post'. He had attended several primary schools, followed by three comprehensive schools. He thought that primary school had been better but that the staff could not handle him. The secondary schools had been a laugh. He remembered, at the first school, coming out of care for a few months, and living with his mum. He had thrown a chair at one of the teachers. His mum went 'down' to school to talk to the head teacher and ended up 'smashing him in the face'. Billy was excluded from school. His mum moved up to London. He eventually started a second comprehensive but hated the lessons, especially French and PE. The teachers hated him too, he claimed, especially the PE teacher, who fancied himself as Bobby Charlton. Billy compared him to the bloke in the film called 'Kes' and concluded that some teachers were more in need of help than the pupils they were asked to assess and label.

Billy was soon in trouble and again 'seen' by social workers, a psychiatrist and educational psychologists, and proudly claimed that his was one of the first Statements of Special Educational Need completed in the capital. He did not think that this had done him any good, however, as it coincided with some more trouble, both in and out of school, even though it did mean he saw a lot more people. He ended up in secure accommodation - a Community Home with Education (CHE) - as well as back in care. His mum disappeared, leaving London.

The placement of Billy at a relatively young age in a secure CHE raises a number of troubling issues, many of which relate to the key themes of punishment, control and welfare, as well as the question of inclusive education. Rayner and Craig (1995) addressed some of these issues in a consideration of secure special education. They asked the basic question, is secure special education either 'safe' or 'secure', both as a form of educational provision, and as an educational or moral construct? Billy's experiences in secure accommodation were less than positive! Is the same true for the many young people who are placed in this provision each year?

A summary of Billy's experience of EBD provision included help from a number of different professionals. The psychiatrist working in a Child Guidance Clinic on the Isle of Wight saw Billy as an infant and diagnosed conduct disorder. Teachers in primary school reported Billy as difficult but unloved, and increasingly given to anti-social behaviour. Their reports consistently highlighted neglect and violence in the home. Later educational reports described further and increasingly serious acting out, involving violence and destruction of property. Academic performance was very poor, although Billy was not identified as having special educational needs. He could read, write and count!

Further assessments by social workers, triggered by an increase of offending incidents, was followed by court reports, which led to the involvement of a guardian *ad litem* as well as a probation officer. This produced further descriptions and accounts of anti-social and criminal behaviour. Concern for Billy's education and care became grounded in managing his behaviour, resulting in a movement away from mainstream education and into special education and care provision.

Billy's perceptions of this assessment and its outcomes makes for sad, yet because of his cynical irony, amusing reading. Clearly much brighter than any of the professionals working with him realised, Billy had been dipping into the literature on psychology in the prison library. He was able to talk informatively about many of the theories underpinning the various diagnoses and interventions intended to help him get back on to the 'right track'. For example, he rejected, albeit tentatively, the psychodynamic ideas of Bowlby (1979; 1988), and suggestions that his behaviour was the result of his lack of breast-feeding, or the absence of his father. He was even more scathingly cynical about a regime based upon behaviour modification and medication in the CHE which, as he recalled, coincided with puberty and other more exciting matters.

Additional assessments by psychiatrists and psychotherapists referred to his psychosexual development, or lack of it, with resulting neuroses, which at the end of the day meant little or nothing at all to Billy. He was equally scathing in his reaction to educational assessments, remembering one young enthusiastic teacher explaining to him that he was stuck in a concrete stage of cognitive development and his difficulties were aggravated by hyperactivity (this was before the discovery of Attention Deficit Disorder). He remembered being quite excited by this revelation at the time, as he recounted how attractive the teacher had been, and how 'close' she got to him, and how he had been able to look up her skirt.

While individual assessment and problem-solving should clearly structure provision for pupils with EBD, it is also important to consider other aspects of educational provision which impact upon the individual. Classroom management, teaching and learning styles, and school-based systems are also part of this equation. A consideration of style differences in learning and behaviour, for example, may offer opportunities to develop pedagogical practice (see Banner & Rayner, 1997; Rayner, 1998; Riding & Rayner, 1998).

The report of a recent DfEE research project investigating EBD provision, policy and practice in mainstream schools provided further evidence that: firstly, effective working with pupils experiencing EBD were linked to corporate realities such as leadership, ethos, shared values, attitudes and aspirations for the education of all pupils, and a shared understanding of EBD; and secondly, that *effective teaching skills for pupils with EBD are the same as those for all pupils'* (Daniels, Visser, Cole & de Reybekill, 1998:1).

This last point is echoed in the words of Fogell and Long (1997:86), who stated that the *'school which makes provision for children with EBD is just like any other school only more so'.* The 'more so', however, perhaps marks only the beginning of a renewed response to the challenge of EBD, which is also reflected in the history of EBD provision. It is, perhaps, timely at this juncture, to suggest that such a response is likely to involve a new concern for what is a fundamental aspect of education, the relationship between teaching and learning, as well as the relationship between teacher(s) and pupils (see Rayner, 1998).

Finally, to more fully appreciate Billy's perspective on the EBD provision which he experienced before ending up in prison, the reader should reflect upon the poem before reading the rest of this chapter (Appendix 1). In Billy's words, his experience had been one of continuous movement, of professionals describing his behaviour by sticking a number of different labels on him. At the end of the day, all of this support and caring, education and intervention, was to leave him facing an uncertain future with 'no home, no job, no dad, and bleeding psychiatrists trying to make him mad'.

Billy's last parting shot was fairly profound. He grinned, as he suggested that there is 'good and bad in all of us' and 'life's grey, not black or white'. It was sensible, therefore, he concluded, that teachers, care staff, and others working with young people with problems should think carefully before labelling a pupil this, that or the other. After all, he opined, 'behind every report, and with every problem, there is a story and a person'. The problem, he suggested, would not be 'fixed' by simply changing the 'surface behaviour'. It was, he argued, very difficult to understand what it meant to experience emotional and behavioural difficulties, but too easy for some people to explain it away, or offer some quick fix solution, or as had happened to him, just to simply blame the individual.

EBD provision - a patchwork quilt or a merry-go-round?
If the desire to respond effectively to EBD is to be realised, it must involve the successful matching of need with resource, and for the involved professional(s), just such an approach and strategy to help manage this requirement is an essential. A useful and simple model of this kind of strategy, reflecting the approach underpinning the SEN *Code of Practice* (DfE, 1994), was presented by Ayers, Clarke and Murray (1995). They described their five-stage procedure as a structured and eclectic model which drew upon various theories and definitions of human behaviour.

The procedure involved five steps:

1. identification of the pupil as a cause for concern;
2. assessment of the pupil's problems;
3. formulation of the pupil's problem or why it happens;
4. intervention or ways of dealing with the problem;
5. evaluation of the intervention.

Clearly, this approach had been used with Billy Bovver at various points during his childhood and adolescence. The result, each time, was to find a placement or make provision for Billy, which was aimed at meeting his needs. The kind or type of provision made would depend upon the way in which original concern was expressed, and to which professional Billy was referred. For example, teachers in primary school tried to cope with Billy, and meet his needs, as simultaneously but separately the Child Guidance Clinic worked with him and attempted to support Billy's mum. More specific assessment and planning may well have helped (see Margerison & Rayner, 1999, for discussion about assessment, targeting and performance tables).

The overall pattern of provision which was available to Billy in his early years reflected that which was organised nationally for young people with EBD. It was, at best, variable in its distribution across the country, and was described in its entirety for the first time by Upton (1983).

Upton initially described this pattern of provision as forming a hierarchical pyramid, made up of medical, special and mainstream schooling. This provision was presented as a dynamic, and perceived as working in an ascending order, moving through an increasingly specialised provision towards a ceiling level comprised of psychiatric units and hospital (see Figure 1).

Topping (1983), focusing more specifically on educational provision, refined this notion of a pyramid, describing a more detailed but similar model to that proposed by Upton. Topping, very significantly, altered Upton's original model of provision. He inverted the pyramid and called it a cascade of provision, reinforcing the notion of a continuum of provision enabling a match with severity of need, but prioritising the preference to maintain a pupil's placement within mainstream education.

HOSPITAL SCHOOLS/UNITS

Children have an identified psychiatric disorder; pathological family circumstances; educational intervention clearly secondary to medical intervention.

RESIDENTIAL SCHOOLS

Difficulty conceived primarily in terms of family pathology; school difficulties common but seen as secondary; children deemed to require long-term and in-depth therapy; children deemed to require a protective environment.

DAY SCHOOLS/SEPARATE UNITS

More extreme school-related problems; home circumstances often unsatisfactory or inadequate, but responsive to support; emphasis upon educational and/or therapeutic help.

SCHOOL-BASED PROVISION

Less extreme problems and primarily related to the school situation; intervention provided primarily through schools, either via the pastoral system or as a curriculum response to educational difficulties; some interventions also in the form of special units with short-term intervention aimed as quick fixes and re-integration into the normal school situation. Emphasis upon 'education as therapy'.

Upton, G. 1983

Figure 1   A hierarchy of educational provision for maladjusted children

At the top of the cascade sat provision which was described as 'within school', and consisted of teacher-based or school-based responses to EBD. These might, for example, include routine sanctions, curriculum reorganisation, strategies for enhancing behaviour management in the classroom or other individual arrangements for a pupil. The DfEE (1997), for example, recommended Assertive Discipline (Canter & Canter, 1992) as one example of this form of provision.

At the other end of the cascade sat residential special school, which was perceived as a last option and reserved for pupils with severe or profound EBD. The dynamic of the system, or movement of pupils within the cascade, therefore, was represented as a progression from 'ordinary class' through to 'total care'. Visser and Rayner have developed this figure by updating it to include recently introduced provision, but retaining the original notion of a cascade of provision (see Figure 2).

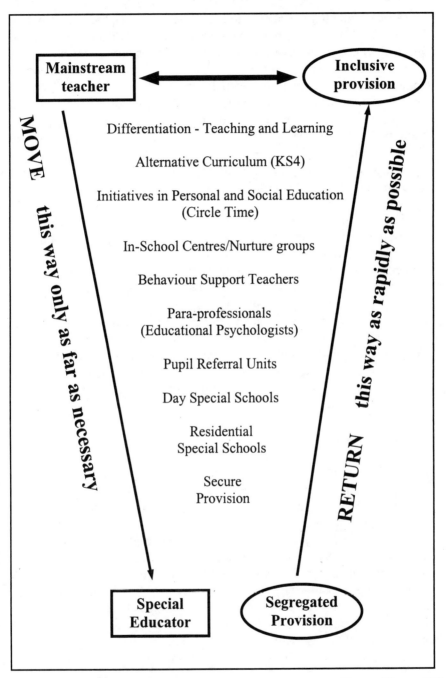

Figure 2   A cascade flow system of EBD provision

Visser and Rayner, 1999
(after Topping, 1983)

More recent attempts at defining the 'system' of EBD provision within England and Wales was made by Cole and Visser (1997). They tried to address some of the issues related to the question of assessing the effectiveness of special schools for pupils with EBD. Drawn from a comprehensive survey of professional views on the nature of EBD and the appropriateness of provision (see, Cole, Visser & Upton, 1988), Cole and Visser extrapolated a range of perspectives which were then superimposed upon established definitions of EBD (see Figure 3). The result is a more complex, indeed messy representation of provision which is probably nearer the reality, perhaps, than the idealised versions proposed by either Upton (1983) or Topping (1983).

While attempting to incorporate notions of internalised problems, or emotional difficulties, with those of externalised problems, or behavioural difficulties, as well as the idea of a continuum of need, reflecting a combination of difficulties ranging from social maladaption to abnormal emotional dysfunction, Cole and Visser (1997) have also tried to parallel the alternative explanations for EBD associated with professional disciplines, including perspectives which are sociological, educational, biophysical and psychiatric. These, indeed, might be further extended to include traditional psychological theories explaining EBD, for example, the psychodynamic, cognitive, behavioural or humanistic perspective (see Cooper, Smith & Upton, 1994; Ayers, Clark & Murray, 1995).

The significance of these various models for the present discussion lies with: first, the way in which an understanding and definition of EBD affects the nature of provision for people identified as experiencing EBD; and second, the way in which the same understanding will frame notions of effectiveness and success. It is a concern for the latter, together with a clearly stated determination to drive up standards in EBD provision, which has apparently influenced recent Government policy (see DfEE, 1997; DfEE, 1999). A single strand running through much of this policy has appeared to be a recognition for multi-disciplinary responses emphasising collaborative work. A need for 'joined-up solutions' reflecting a more co-ordinated approach to 'social exclusion', and to EBD, is reflected in recent legislation and guidance. For the reader interested in this aspect of provision, reading on the subject of truancy and school attendance offers a very good start, particularly Carlen (1992).

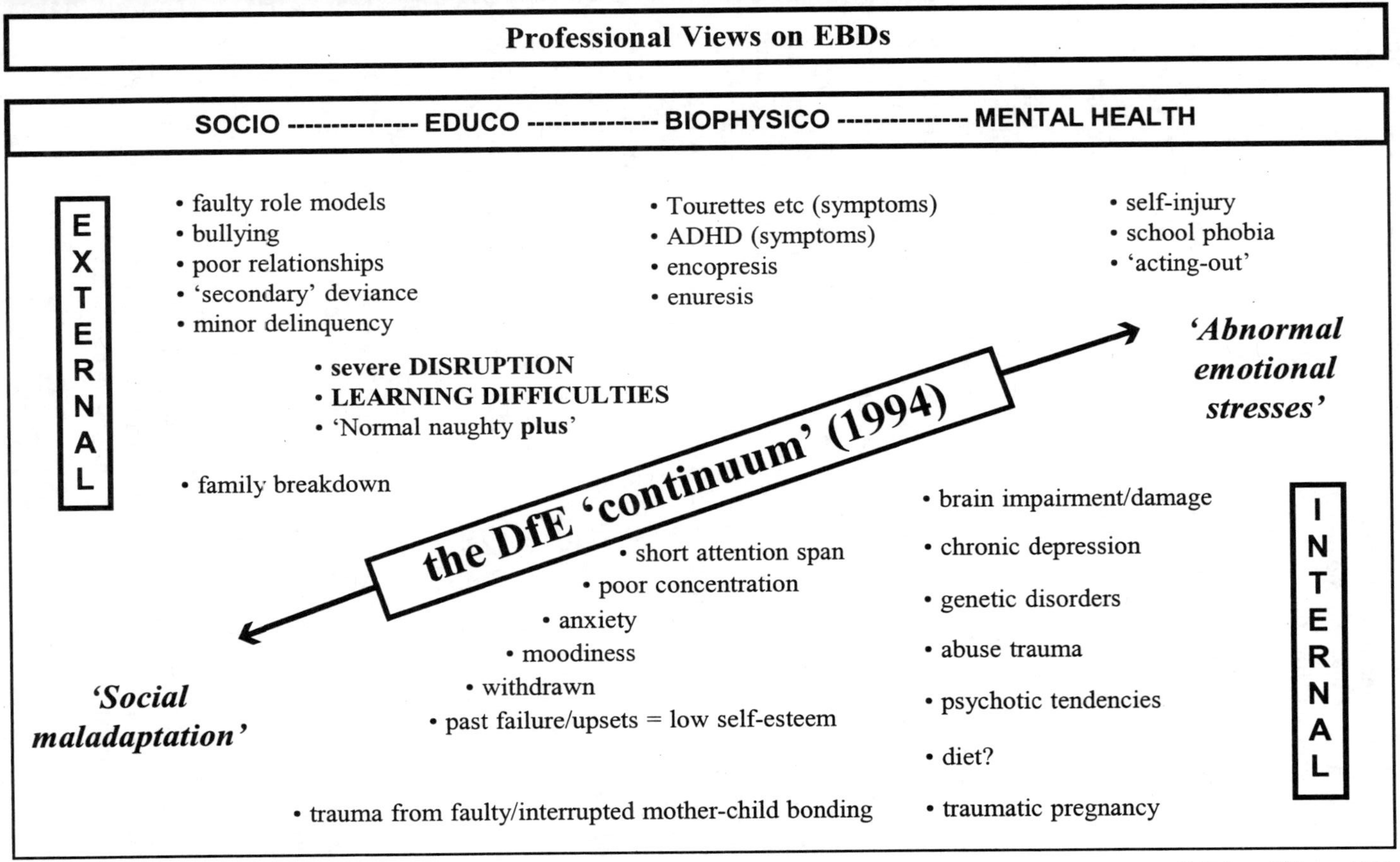

Professional Views on EBDs

SOCIO ----------- EDUCO ----------- BIOPHYSICO ----------- MENTAL HEALTH

EXTERNAL

- faulty role models
- bullying
- poor relationships
- 'secondary' deviance
- minor delinquency

- family breakdown

- trauma from faulty/interrupted mother-child bonding

'Social maladaptation'

- severe DISRUPTION
- LEARNING DIFFICULTIES
- 'Normal naughty plus'

the DfE 'continuum' (1994)

- short attention span
- poor concentration
- anxiety
- moodiness
- withdrawn
- past failure/upsets = low self-esteem

- Tourettes etc (symptoms)
- ADHD (symptoms)
- encopresis
- enuresis

- brain impairment/damage
- chronic depression
- genetic disorders
- abuse trauma
- psychotic tendencies
- diet?
- traumatic pregnancy

- self-injury
- school phobia
- 'acting-out'

'Abnormal emotional stresses'

INTERNAL

© Cole and Visser, 1997

Figure 3   Professional views and effective EBD provision

27

The emphasis upon multi-agency provision for young people with EBD is reflected in recent legislation. For example, in the *Education Act 1996*, a duty was placed upon the LEA to prepare a plan setting out arrangements for the education of children with EBD. The LEA, furthermore, was required to consider how their plans related to those of other services within the local authority. Behaviour support plans have been developed in the past 12 months or more, which seek to pull together not only the educational provision for EBD, but to also link it to the related non-educational provision for the same children, with the intention that all provision should be co-ordinated and complementary.

A second example is provided by the more recent draft guidance entitled, 'Social Inclusion: Pupil Support' (DfEE, 1999), signalling even further Government determination to achieve better co-ordinated responses to EBD across a range of services as part of an attempt to produce a seamless provision for children with EBD. The guidance, prepared in conjunction with the Department of Health, Home Office and Social Exclusion Unit, was intended as a single document, drawing together the law relating to attendance, pupil behaviour and discipline, the use of exclusion and education out of school. Furthermore, the guidance was explicitly intended to offer 'practical advice' on strategies for early intervention and prevention of EBD through 'multi-agency working'.

The rightness of this approach is not questioned by the writer. If the educational and personal needs of an individual identified as experiencing EBD are to be met, it is an imperative that better multi-agency working is realised. Indeed, even within school, the notion of a corporate approach reflected in whole-school policies, and a team-based implementation of school discipline and behaviour management is further demonstration of the importance for teachers of collaboration and peer support. The importance of this point cannot be exaggerated - as every professional who has worked in a special school (EBD) would no doubt testify. It is certainly the case that if EBD provision is to contain depth as well as breadth, it must involve multi-agency work.

A note of caution should be expressed here, however, as it is very easy for a multi-agency approach involving a number of well-meaning professionals surrounding a young person to confuse and be confusing to that person. The result is very often an individual with a history of being 'moved from pillar to post', exhibiting many behaviours which might more easily be explained by lack of security and stability than by more orthodox explanations for EBD. The potential for conflict and fragmented intervention becomes alarmingly obvious as consideration is given to the number of interventions associated with different professionals and their theoretical perspectives (see Davie, 1993, for a useful and far-sighted discussion of this issue).

The very real dangers of overwhelming the individual being supported mean that ensuring effective inter-agency support is a considerable challenge. It also involves teachers embracing a wider notion of education than that of a traditional commitment to teaching a subject within the four walls of the classroom. The danger of ineffective provision is obvious, the risk of future harm to the individual alarming, and the significant chance of placement and provision being organised on the basis of serendipity rather sad.

Yet, it is equally clear that long-term success in meeting the needs of young people experiencing EBD will be dependent upon responses from a number of professionals across a range of provision. It is, nevertheless, a considerable challenge to those involved, if they are to prevent EBD provision merely forming a merry-go-round of placement and experience.

The notion of a patchwork quilt of provision comprising successful joint-agency work is one possible model of effective EBD provision. Earlier writers addressing the question of EBD provision tended to perceive it, somewhat negatively, as such a patchwork (Cooling, 1974), or even a 'rag-bag' of different provision (Laslett, 1977). Perhaps historically, this variation in pattern is a necessary first step towards building provision which will become less patchwork and more seamless in its make-up, as further development of working practice across a range of services is attempted. The kind of approach envisaged is outlined in Unit 2, reflecting the proposals made by one LEA in their Behaviour Support Plan (Wolverhampton LEA, 1999).

The need to place the individual first and foremost at the heart of the process of planning and delivering provision is perhaps self-evident. It is to be hoped that LEA Behaviour Support Plans will reflect this principle as a stated intention. For the purpose of this discussion, it is also useful to reconsider some of the key themes identified at the start of this chapter and the question of effective EBD provision through the example of Billy Bovver's story of being a 'malad'.

Early years provision - prevention is better than a cure
While early intervention need not necessarily mean work with infants
and children, but may refer to prompt responses to problems presented by
teenagers or young people experiencing EBD for the first time, it is
generally associated with early years provision. Early intervention for
Billy included medical support through the Child Guidance Clinic and
educational support aimed at helping him to develop within the school
context. Psychiatrists and psychologists worked with Billy; the first found
Billy suffering with conduct disorder and hyperactivity, the latter
concluded that a cognitive impairment and personality dysfunction was
preventing normal development. The latter recommended behaviour
modification in a secure setting, thereby enabling a clinical application of
behaviour management and medication.

The *purpose* of early intervention in Billy's life was for the most part
about treating him for a cure. Punishment did not feature greatly, but
welfare and education played an important part in provision which sought
to understand Billy, compensate for the things missing in his life, and in
Billy's words, attempted to 'nag him into conformity'. Psychiatric
provision merely resulted in a label, and a series of consultations in the
clinic.

The *principles* underpinning this approach were child-centred, but
deficit-based, and either saw Billy's needs as psychological, determined
by parental separation and neglect, or the result of clinical disorders
which required psychiatric treatment. The problem, however, was Billy's,
and Billy needed to be changed. Alternative *placement*, however, did not
involve specialised location, but instead, interventions aimed at
supporting and maintaining Billy in the home and community. The action
of separating infants from their parents, if at all possible, was clearly to be
avoided.

In Billy's story, there is no evidence that early *intervention* worked -
that is, matching stated policy and provision with professional praxis.
There was no suggestion of collaboration between Child Guidance and
school. The role of parents was not emphasised. The question of
provision - more particularly of inclusion and exclusion - does not appear
to have been raised. Yet, ironically, it is probably true that Billy would
have been more likely excluded from primary school if this pattern of
problems had occurred during the last decade (see Hayden, 1997; Castle

and Parsons, 1997). This fact, together with alarming increases in numbers of pupils being excluded, has clearly influenced recent Government policy emphasising inclusion (see DfEE, 1997).

Research in this area was developed over a considerable period by Chazan and co-workers, reflecting an interest in the social development of early years children in school. Chazan, Laing, Harper and Bolton (1983), for example, drew upon a large survey to explore difficulties presented by young children and the question of developing forms of appropriate provision and effective intervention. Latterly, recent work by Chazan, Laing, Davies and Phillips (1998) focused more specifically on helping children and adolescents who are withdrawn or socially isolated.

A further development of interest, reflecting the same priority upon early years found in the Government policy, is the work of Bennathan and Boxall (1996). This work described the introduction and development of 'nurture groups' for very young children. The difficulties presented by many children were perceived to be the result of negative experiences in the home, caused by inadequacies in child-rearing practice. Children increasingly, the writers argued, were entering school without the 'concepts, skills and controls' necessary for success. One is tempted to add 'life' or 'society' to this argument.

Nurture groups were therefore formed to target these pupils and provide child-centred strategies for teachers, who were charged with organising activities which emphasised play and routine. In Bennathan's words, children in these groups experienced '... in essence ordinary primary school teaching but slowed down to the rate that the child could absorb' (Bennathan, 1997). There is a temptation to wonder whether much of Billy's early difficulties might have benefited by this kind of specialised targeting within the school classroom.

A third approach aimed at the primary phase of education and intended to focus even more closely on school-based provision is described by Fairhurst and Riding (1995). These writers have developed a simple but effective framework for teaching the skills of behaviour management to parents, in collaboration with school. Given the recent introduction of home-school agreements, this kind of approach is likely to have increasing appeal to teachers (see sections 100 and 111 of the *School Standards and Framework Act 1998*).

Later provision - cascading down the pyramid

Other professionals were subsequently involved in administering further assessments and diagnoses for Billy's condition or behaviour. A number of explanations for Billy's emotional and behaviour difficulties were offered, including several new labels such as 'delinquent' and 'psychopath'. Theories offered included a neurologist's explanation that Billy seemed to have physical deformities to his brain, motivational dysfunction, and waywardness. Alternatively, other theories suggested that it was not Billy to blame, but the environment, and more specifically the social or ecosystems surrounding Billy, and not least, those occurring within school.

In terms of provision, however, Billy seemed to spend an increasing amount of time in and out of care, after initially being placed in a CHE on a psychologist's recommendation that he follow an individual treatment plan. Billy subsequently travelled along a predictable 'career route' through the rest of his school-time, comprising a 'mix' or 'merry-go-round' of educational and care provision, involving mainstream education, foster placement, secure accommodation, residential special schooling, and eventually, full-time incarceration in prison.

Billy's secondary schooling involved him in a number of different placements, reflecting the patchwork nature of EBD provision. At the same time, Billy experienced a slide down the continuum cascade identified by Topping (1983). A number of different interventions, often grounded in competing ideologies, were unsuccessfully attempted. Billy, for example, was sent off to a boarding school. This provision was organised around a child-centred philosophy which sought to emulate that developed in a therapeutic community.

Billy was exposed to principles which reflected a psychodynamic theory. Psychotherapy, for instance, organised within the curriculum, involved a specialist employed to work with the children. Billy, more astute than those working with him at the time realised, understood some of this approach, having read some texts describing Freudian theory, the work of Anna Freud, and Klein's ideas about defence mechanisms and psychosis (see Greenhalgh, 1994, for a very good interpretation of the place of psychodynamic theories in the school curriculum). Billy was not impressed and looking back thought that none of it had worked for him.

While the experience of residential school was not helpful as far as Billy was concerned (Billy inferred that he had experienced some sexual abuse there), and with the emphasis increasingly on inclusion, the place and usefulness of removal and segregation to a special community is not necessarily to be dismissed. Several authors have lamented the demise of residential provision (Rose, 1993; Chaplain & Freeman, 1994) and Cole, Visser and Upton (1998) alert the reader to the need for such provision. Indeed, while those who are uncertain about the role of residential provision should read Chaplain and Freeman's useful analysis of 'caring under pressure', those who would dismiss therapeutic provision and the theory of psychodynamic development could do worse than read Rose's passionate account of life in a therapeutic community (Rose, 1993).

The key themes of punishment, welfare and education appear and reappear in this part of Billy's story. Attempts made by workers in a range of provision reflect a range of value positions, attitudes and beliefs about EBD. One explanation involved Kahn's theory of 'long chromosomes and a translocated gene', another Malliphant's theory of 'recidivism', and yet another alternative view that this individual is a 'psychopath'. Much of this theory failed to inform practice or provision. One is tempted to ask how could it? Certainly, there seemed little evidence of thought-out principles structuring provision, and there seemed little match between competing ideology.

Taken together, the story makes for a confused pattern of variation and fragmentation which fails to match stated policy and provision with professional praxis. The only consistent themes in Billy's story appear to be the steady increase in specialisation reflecting the steady lack of success with intervention, and the movement towards segregation not inclusion. It is interesting to note Cole's observation (Cole, 1989), that the number of pupils statemented for EBD and placed in special educational provision continued to rise during the 1980s - will the figures tell a similar story at the end of this present decade?

The sad truth, however, is that none of this provision 'met Billy's needs', in so far as it helped to prevent further difficulty, or resolve some of the difficulties facing Billy at the time. Even locking Billy up was less than successful, given that he used the time to learn new criminal skills, which when later applied, resulted in his ending up in prison. The implication of all of this, considered in wider terms socially and educationally, is that EBD provision then and now may be less than effective. Yet, the problems are mounting, in terms of the numbers, frequency and severity of EBD. Cooper (1998), for instance, has pointed out that several forms of EBD have shown an alarming increase since 1945.

Cooper (1998), furthermore, noted that recorded criminal offences signalled an increase, by a factor of seven, of juvenile delinquency in this country. He also pointed to a rise in the incidence of psychosocial problems, albeit many of which had attracted new labels such as 'oppositional defiant disorder'as well as some related to previously used labels (conduct disorder). Generally, however, Cooper concluded that evidence was available to suggest a continuing rise in the severity and frequency of young people experiencing severe emotional difficulties such as clinical depression and sexual trauma. Socially, similar problems were also reflected in the extraordinary rise of school exclusion, and a more widespread increase in social exclusion. Clearly, for those decision-makers responsible for making policy and managing provision, the vexed question of effectiveness must remain a priority and a challenge.

Conclusion

The ultimate purpose of EBD provision is the education of young people through meeting their needs and enabling their personal, intellectual and social development. It is also a presumption that such educational provision will involve interventions which will have a therapeutic effect, contributing to a resolution of EBD. The questions then posed, however, are, how appropriate is such placement and how well is it managed?

This question of purpose, often reflected in an emphasis between care and education, welfare and discipline, or moral and legal principles of right and wrong, has historically illustrated how perspectives and an understanding of EBD have shaped provision (see Cole, 1986; Cole, 1989; Rayner, 1999). Clearly, stated aims will enable professionals to measure success, and perhaps quality, and to this end, purpose is a prerequisite for realising achievement. It is therefore important to regularly evaluate the appropriateness of provision.

An alternative way of considering the same question of overall effectiveness, however, is to focus more specifically upon management of provision. A simple way of attempting this exercise is to apply the 'triple E test' (Rayner, 1997). This involves measuring provision in terms of its effectiveness, efficiency and equity. If provision is *effective* - it will achieve desired results and realise worthwhile aims previously identified. If provision is *efficient* - it will reflect an optimum resource match and obtain maximum results with the available potential. If provision is *equitable* - it will be fairly and viably organised and ensure an equality of opportunity.

The issue of effectiveness has been the central focus in this chapter. It is equally important, however, to consider issues related to efficiency and equity. For example, how have individual differences been accommodated in past and present EBD provision? Are there inequities of provision related to gender and race differences? A second set of questions related to both equity and efficiency are resource-based and involve finance. Does EBD provision pay? Is there value for money in the various arrangements which exist to meet the needs of pupils with EBD? Furthermore, whose needs are being met in the present arrangement? Topping (1990) considered this kind of approach in a relevant updating of his earlier work on EBD provision, and focused upon the issue of cost-effectiveness.

Cole, Visser and Upton (1998) have made a start in examining some of these issues as they have impacted upon EBD special schools. They proposed a notion of 'proficient provision' to describe an arrangement which was 'appropriate' and 'worked' for pupils with EBD. They identified key elements which were found to be in place in provision judged to be an example of good practice, and which the writer suggests, reflected a successful management of effectiveness, efficiency and equity.

Proficient provision was characterised by key features such as the existence of comprehensive *policies* which were implemented and regularly reviewed; differentiated individual educational plans and care plans which targeted both intellectual and personal development; and an educational environment and ethos which valued various social needs and relationships both within and outside of the school. Cole, Visser and Upton (1998) argued that dissemination of such good practice and a greater awareness of proficiency at all levels of provision would greatly contribute to a genuine inclusive education. Perhaps, but what is helpful here is the notion of careful consideration of provision, and the need to reconsider not only its effectiveness, but also its efficiency and equity.

The question of value and worth when considering EBD provision, generally, is very complicated. Difficulties related to definition and organisation, perceptions and values, attitudes and policy, all combine to underline the nature of an enterprise which is, perhaps ironically, quintessentially problematic. The very nature of EBD is paradoxical. It is a phenomenon that is both subjective and objective, personal and social, emotional and intellectual, and ultimately, it is a construct which is relative and contextual. Making, managing and measuring EBD provision was never likely to be easy. Nevertheless, questions of effectiveness, efficiency and equity must be answered by those who are responsible as policy and practice is developed to promote an inclusive education for children and young people with EBD.

BALLAD OF A MALAD

My name is Billy Bovver
I'm a modern day young man
I wear me Doctor Martins
And I'll groin you if I can.
Me father was a boozer
I'm afraid he often swore
Me mother it is rumoured
An unsuccessful whore.
She fed me on the bottle
'Cos I had a violent suck
She had some great big Bristols
I never had much luck.
She toilet trained me easy
She used a pad and bell
But I stopping peeing anyway
I couldn't stand the smell.
Mum sent me off to playschool
To learn to get on with me peers
I cried loudly when she left me
Full of separation fears.
But playschool it was caring
Though they killed off my pet louse
Playing mums and daddies
Lying in the Wendy House.
I was brung up on the Isle of Wight
Interviewed by Rutter
Psychiatric diagnosis
Said I was a little nutter.

My first teacher in the junior school
Thought I was a likely lad
She hugged me to her bosom
Like my mother never had.
All the teachers they were women
Thought that Bowlby was their saviour
But they nagged me when I mucked about
Couldn't handle male behaviour.
Me father he got 15 years
He said it was a doddle
But I just had to soldier on
Without a real male model.
I then went to the local Comp
It was a right old laff

Just think of 15,000 hours
Spent mostly in the caff.
I hated doing history
At maths I comes a cropper
I hated doing rotten French
I can't speak English proper.
The Head he then then referred me
He said I was a yob
My mother didn't quite agree
And smashed him in the gob.

A crisis with a task
But I would have put him right
He only had to ask.
Minuchin said it's chaos
His family is sick
So how come se sibs are free
While I'm here in the nick.

Weinberg said masked depression
Enuresis was his backing
But recent research data
Shows his theory sadly-lacking.
The neurologist said limbic
Hypothatamus and lesion
Cerebral inequality
And me mum a right old Fresian.
Mowrer said "he's just frustrated
He's never reached his goal
He's only fit for prison
Or digging down a hole".
Eysenck said "he's unstable
A large N and P and E".
Binet found me retarded
A mental age of 3
The systems men said it's the school
Crumby organisation
But they won't change the teachers
With their views of deprivation.
And self-fulfilling prophecy
Modifies class interaction
I must admit a caning
Never gave *me* satisfaction.

Hersov säid "he's a school phobic
Of teachers he's a dread
He needs some care and loving
And hitting around the head".
Herbert said "that's stupid
It's only S and R's
Modify his situation
Put him behind some bars".

This fuss about me reading
The teachers had some gall
The only thing I like to read
Is jon the bog 'ole wall.
Piaget said a concrete kid
Won't reach the formal stage
But I don't think that logic
Will earn a decent wage.
Some tart said hyperactive
She proved it to the hilt
My pulse rate it shot straight up
I could see right up her kilt.

I met a bloke called Ravenette
Who tried to save my soul
He only found three constructs
Sex, drugs and rock 'n' roll.

A psychologist's assessment
Found cognition sadly lacking
'Cos I didn't like to play with blocks
Knew nothing 'bout meat packing.
They said I's disadvantaged
My family life was hell
So they sent me off to Stamford House
And looked me in a cell.
They tried to stop my aggro
By trying behaviour mod
Every time that I was naughty
They said "you little sod".
They controlled my extraversion
With little pills of blue
I was doped up to the eyeballs
Better than a tube of glue.

I then went to a CHE
Which used the buddy system
But my buddy he got locked away
For playing with my piston.
My masturbating tendencies
Were stopped by my girl Lyn
I almost liked having her
As much as the real thing.
I then got caught for nicking lead
Clark said "the situation
gave him the chance to do it"
So I only got probation.

I liked the I.T. unit
Fixing motors every day
The knowledge that they gave me
Got me done for T.D.A.
They tried the short sharp shock on me
But I'd heard of Douglas Bader
If a legless man can handle it
They'd have to hit me harder.
The socios said "poor young mug
He has a cultural gap"
An illness of society
But I've never had the clap.

Old Sigmund said I's anal
He was a stupid yid
To know of child psychiatry
From seeing just one kid.
Young Anna she was better
Though a trifle circumspectual
She said I liked to knock things off
Sublimating something sexual.
Klein said unconscious fantasies
Defences and psychosis
But if you had to ask me
She envied my neurosis.
Erikson said identify
They classed me as a criminal
The label, well it hurt
Even psychs they cheat and lie
Just think of Cyril Burt.

Kahn said me chromosomes are long
A translocated gene
He made it sound like I'd two heads
A Martian that was green,
West said "it's social learning
He's got it from his peers".
So they sent me off to boarding school
To learn to live with queers.
Schachter said a psychopath

Aroused most every day
The only blokes I knew like that
Was Ron and Reggie Kray.
The Gluecks's Prediction Table
Their theory I would knock it
They only knew I was a thief
When I tried to pick their pocket.
Maliphant said "he's recidivist
He's done it all before
We'll cure his impulsivity
And nail him to the floor".
The do-good social worker
This image is a kid
They lock up more young people
Than Hitler ever did
Now Norman Tutt's a guy I like
He knows 'bout institutions
Their failure to effect a change
With half thought out solutions.

I've been labelled as delinquent
Disadvantaged male pubescent
Deprived high-tempo layabout
A turmoiled adolescent.
Extravert and psychopathic
My home unsatisfactory
Pushed around by caring birds.
No wonder I'm refractory.

So what will become of me
No home, no job, no dad
These bleedin' psychiatrists
Trying to make me mad.
There's good and bad in all of us
I'm sure you'll think that right
So think before you label
Life's grey, not black or white.
A growing lad needs action
He wants to try things out
His own self he is seeking
Authority he'll flout.
So at the end my message
Is that I'm well, not ill
I might well just grown out of it
In fact I think I will.

References

Ayers, H., Clarke, D. and Murray, A. (1995) *Perspectives on Behaviour: a practical guide to effective interventions for teachers.* London: David Fulton.

Banner, G. and Rayner, S. (1997) 'Teaching with Style: making the difference!' *Support for Learning,* Vol 12, 1, pp 15-18.

Bennathan, M. (1997) 'Effective Intervention in Primary Schools: what nurture groups achieve.' *Emotional and Behavioural Difficulties,* Vol 2, 3, 23-29.

Bennathan, M. and Boxall, M. (1996) *Effective Intervention in Primary Schools - Nurture Groups.* London: David Fulton.

Bowlby, J. (1979) *The Making and Breaking of Affectionate Bonds.* London: Routledge.

Bowlby, J. (1988) *A Secure Base: Clinical Application of Attachment Theory.* London: Routledge.

Canter, L. and Canter, M. (1992) *Assertive Discipline: Positive Behaviour Management for Today's Classroom* (2nd Edition). Santa Monica, CA: Canter Associates.

Carlen, P. (1992) *The Politics of Compulsory Schooling,* Milton Keynes: Open University Press.

Castle, F. and Parsons, C. (1997) 'Disruptive Behaviour and Exclusions from School: redefining and responding.' *Emotional and Behavioural Difficulties,* Vol 2, 3, 4-11.

Chaplain, R. and Freeman, A. (1994) *Caring Under Pressure.* London: David Fulton.

Chazan, M., Laing, A. F., Davies, D. and Phillips, R. (1998) *Helping Socially Withdrawn and Isolated Children and Adolescents.* London: Cassell.

Chazan, M., Laing, A. F., Harper, G. C. and Bolton, J. (1983) *Helping Young Children with Behaviour Difficulties.* London: Croom Helm.

Cole, T. (1986) *Residential Special Education.* Milton Keynes: Open University Press.

Cole, T. (1989) *Apart or A Part? Integration and the Growth of British Special Education.* Milton Keynes: Open University Press.

Cole T. and Visser, J. (1997). *Lecture Notes and Publication being completed (EDSE 06). EBD Course.* Birmingham: University of Birmingham.

Cole, T., Visser, J., and Upton, G. (1998) *Effective Schooling for Pupils with Emotional and Behavioural Difficulties.* London: David Fulton.

Cooling, M. (1974) *Educational Provision for Maladjusted Children in Boarding Schools in England and Wales.* M.Ed. Thesis. Liverpool: The University of Liverpool.

Cooper, P. (1998) 'Developments in the Understanding of Childhood Emotional and Behavioural Problems since 1981.' In R. Laslett, P. Cooper, P. Maras, A. Rimmer and B. Law. *Changing Perceptions: Emotional and Behavioural Difficulties since 1945.* East Sutton: AWCEBD.

Cooper, P., Smith, C. and Upton, G. (1994) *Emotional and Behavioural Difficulties.* London: Routledge.

Daniels, H., Visser, J., Cole, T. and de Reybekill, N. (1999) *Emotional and Behavioural Difficulties in Mainstream Schools*. London: DfEE Publications.

Davie, R. (1993) 'Assessing and understanding children's behaviour.' Chapter 3. In T. Charlton and K. David (Eds) *Managing Misbehaviour*. London: Macmillan.

Department for Education (1994) *A Code of Practice for the Identification and Assessment of Special Educational Needs*. London: HMSO.

Department for Education and Employment (1997) *Excellence in Schools*. London: DfEE.

Department for Education and Employment (1999) *Draft Guidance on Social Inclusion: Pupil Support*. London: DfEE.

Fairhurst. P. and Riding, R. J. (1995) *Better Behaviour: A Guide to Behavioural and Emotional Problems*. Birmingham: Learning and Training Technology.

Fogell, J. and Long, R. (1997) *Emotional and Behavioural Difficulties*. Tamworth: NASEN.

Greenhalgh, P. (1994) *Emotional Growth and Learning*. London: Routledge.

Hayden, C. (1997) 'Exclusion from Primary School: children "in need" and children with 'special educational need.' *Emotional and Behavioural Difficulties*, Vol 2, 3, 36-44.

Laslett, R. (1977) *Educating Maladjusted Children*. London: Granada.

Margerison, A. and Rayner, S. (1999) 'Troubling Targets and School Needs: Assessing behaviour in the classroom.' *Support for Learning, Vol 14, No 2, 87-92.*

Rayner (1997) Lecture Notes: The Management of Special Education. School of Education: University of Birmingham.

Rayner, S. G. (1998) 'Educating Pupils with Emotional and Behaviour Difficulties: Pedagogy is the Key!' *Emotional and Behavioural Difficulties*, Vol 3, 2, 39-47.

Rayner, S. G. (1999) *EDSE 06, Unit 2, Emotional and Behaviour Difficulties: Policy, Practice and Provision*. Distance Education Course Material. Birmingham: University of Birmingham.

Rayner, S., and Craig, P. (1995) 'Secure Special Education: is it safe or sound?' *Emotional and Behavioural Difficulties*, Vol 4, 3, 44-51.

Riding, R. J. and Rayner, S. (1998) *Cognitive Styles and Learning Strategies*. London: David Fulton.

Rose, M. (1993) *The Trouble with Teenagers - a guide to caring for disturbed adolescents*. London: Positive Publication.

Topping, K. (1990) *Disruptive Pupils: Changes in Perception and Provision*. In M. Scherer, I. Gersch. and L. Fry. (Eds) *Meeting Disruptive Behaviour*. Basingstoke: MacMillan Ed.

Topping, K.S. (1983) *Educational Systems for Disruptive Adolescents*. London: Croom Helm.

Upton, G. (1983) *Educating Children with Behaviour Problems*. Cardiff: Faculty of Education, University College, Cardiff.

Wolverhampton LEA (1999) *Behaviour Support Plan, 1999-2000*. Wolverhampton: Wolverhampton LEA.

Chapter Three

Accepting Diversity: refocusing interventions over EBD

by Paul Howard

In this chapter, I will examine some of the underlying problems in many contemporary interventions in respect of pupils' emotional and behavioural difficulties (EBD). Although in recent years the special school sector has not contracted in absolute terms, mainstream schools have grown dramatically in importance, as settings in which EBD, along with other special educational needs, are recognised, a trend which is graphically demonstrated in the Green Paper, *Excellence for all children* (DfEE, 1997). During the same period, governmental responses have increasingly been informed by a shift in emphasis from individuals to professional practice, as indicated in the Green Paper, and *The Action Programme for SEN* (DfEE, 1998a), which it spawned. Reflecting these trends, the chapter is written on the assumption that the key interests in the EBD field are now unarguably of relevance to *all* educational settings.

In the changing context of responses to EBD, the *Code of Practice for the Identification and Assessment of Special Educational Needs* (DfE, 1994a) can be regarded as a watershed. Whereas pupils with EBD had been present in mainstream schools prior to its introduction and their inclusion encouraged to some extent by previous SEN legislation (DES 1981), the *Code of Practice* has provided schools with a coherent rationale for identifying an increasing number of pupils as experiencing and presenting EBD. As the prospect of securing additional resources for intervention has come to be associated with the statutory responsibilities of LEAs, which, even in the delegationist climate engendered by 'Fair Funding' (DfEE, 1998b), has not diminished, it is not surprising that the *Code of Practice* has acted as a conveyor belt moving towards formal assessment and Statementing at the earliest opportunity.

In the process, the definition of 'EBD', which has never been straightforward, has become all the more difficult. Responding to the difficulty of definition, the authors of Circular 9/94 concluded that:

> '... children with EBD[1] are on a continuum. Their problems are clearer and greater than sporadic naughtiness or

moodiness and yet not so great as to be classed as mental illness'.

(DfE, 1994b)

[1] The use of the term 'with EBD' is used throughout for convenience and is not intended to convey a pathological view of those difficulties.

The breadth of definition embraced in this conclusion is both its strength and its weakness. On the one hand, few would dispute that a diversity of difficulty, from very withdrawn behaviour to excessive acting out, can be validated as 'EBD'. On the other, the very vagueness of definition has resulted in an apparently ever-growing number of pupils being drawn into the EBD net. This is not to suggest that adult, especially teacher, perceptions of pupils' difficulties are without foundation, but that the breadth of official definitions of EBD has helped support an assumption of logical, perhaps inevitable, progression from initial concern about behaviour to the articulation of formally assessed EBD, possibly with less questioning of what can be done to address the concern.

Despite its impact in terms of the numbers of pupils identified as having EBD, the *Code of Practice* may not have stimulated much diversity of approach to those difficulties in mainstream schools, where a significant majority of responses has been informed, admittedly often loosely, by a behaviourist perspective, in so far as they have a theoretical underpinning at all. The correlation between the Code and the behaviourist orientation of many school-based interventions can be traced in the emphasis on:

- objective observation of pupil behaviours;
- articulation of inappropriate behaviours;
- target-setting (most prominently through Individual Education Plans) for improved behaviour;
- changing pupil behaviour.

All of which apparently dovetails into the predominant culture of education in general, which, through a sequence of legislation during the last ten years or so, has cemented the centrality of testing, target-setting and outputs.

Although the orientation of behaviourist interventions in response to EBD is, thus, compatible with the contemporary culture in education as a whole, the relationship is not without tension. With schools under an increasing pressure to perform against normative criteria and facing

43

penalties for failure, the perceived propensity of 'difficult pupils' to impede that performance can result in their removal being seen as more beneficial than concerted efforts to address their needs. However gloomy an interpretation this might seem, one only need look at the proportion of pupils with assessed EBD in the explosion in permanent exclusions to conclude that it has some validity. Even in Authorities with relatively low levels of exclusion, pupils with EBD are disproportionately represented in the excluded cohort.

In short, the consequences of a school failing to meet targets (being placed on special measures, named or shamed or located in the relegation zone of a performance league table) are mirrored in the consequences of individual pupils' failure. As far as pupils with EBD are concerned, these consequences are no doubt more striking than for others. At the heart of this problem is a widespread difficulty, in both mainstream and special schools, in sustaining the recognition of EBD as special educational needs. Although their passage through the stages of the *Code of Practice* in mainstream settings may be identical to that of their peers with other learning difficulties, pupils with EBD often have a qualitatively different experience of the target-setting which is integral to the process. Whereas other pupils' IEPs invariably serve to validate the achievement of small steps forward, for pupils with EBD they frequently delineate the leap which they are expected to make. Thus, pupils with EBD are most likely to be called upon to demonstrate significant gains in the very areas in which they have been assessed as having marked difficulty.

At its most punitive, this phenomenon can be likened to a high jump competition in which the opening height is set at one centimetre above the current world record. If the pupil with EBD cannot comply with *all* the behavioural expectations of the school, their progress against *any* of those expectations is invalidated and failure guaranteed. Were this stance replicated across the SEN board, its equivalence might be to require a non-reader to complete *War and Peace* in a single sitting.

On first impressions, the SEN Green Paper (DfEE, 1997) appears to tackle the adverse differentiation of EBD from other types of learning difficulty, by devoting a whole chapter to EBD. However, this welcomed recognition has to be set against the almost total omission of reference to EBD in any of the other, more general chapters. Moreover, the footprints in the sand of the Green Paper have not survived the incoming tide of the

Programme of Action (DfEE, 1998a), which makes no significant mention of EBD. Once again, the ambiguous status of EBD in relation to special educational needs appears to have been confirmed. As a consequence of this distinct way of framing EBD, there is often a pronounced inclination towards normalisation.

Recent research by the University of Birmingham concludes that among the characteristics of mainstream schools, which respond effectively to pupils with EBD, is the capacity to accommodate diversity, for example, by differentiation within the pastoral system (Daniels, Visser, Cole & de Reybekill, 1998).

Elsewhere, possibly in the majority of schools, the underlying assumption seems to be that the uniform treatment of all pupils secures 'normal' behaviour. It is a 'one cap fits all' mentality, which makes little or no allowance for the diversity of behaviours, emotions and learning patterns which are 'normal', let alone those which fall within the continuum that is described as 'EBD'.

Where approaches to pupils' EBD deny their diversity, it is difficult to see how they can contribute to the process of increasing inclusion as set out in the Green Paper and *Programme of Action*. That the accommodation of diversity lies at the centre of inclusive educational practice is widely documented (Forest & Pearpoint, 1992; Clark, Dyson & Milward, 1995; Rouse & Florian, 1996) and, therefore, there is a strong case for ensuring that inclusive principles inform all responses to pupils with EBD. These principles clearly go deeper than the question of school placement, for where inclusion does not rise above the issue of location it will tend to be impoverished and contribute to a closed model. Distinctions between closed and open models of inclusion may be summarised thus:

Features of Closed Model	Features of Open Model
Concerned with location of education	Concerned with quality of education
Focus on small minority of pupils	Focus on all pupils
Focus on pupils' EBD	Focus also on behaviour of staff and others associated with school
Concerned with 'learning difficulty'	Concerned with learning and teaching
Individual focus only	Institutional focus as well

Table 1: Comparison of Closed and Open Models of Inclusion

Although the distinction may never be as clear-cut as the representation in Table 1 (it may be more accurate to view each of the pairs of statements as points towards opposite ends of a spectrum), there is no doubt that the benefits for pupils with EBD are greater when intervention is guided by open principles. Among the features of what I have termed an 'open model of inclusion' are two of the strongest insurances of appropriate and effective interventions in response to pupils' EBD, the inclusion of adult behaviours and of an institutional gaze. These are no less relevant to special schools than they are to mainstream settings.

With or without the identification of certain pupils as having EBD, mainstream schools are complex settings and their complexity tends to preclude the rigorous application of a behaviourist perspective. Whereas in small special schools, units or clinics, it may be possible to control conditions, this is not the case where the customary group size is around 30 and the population in the hundreds or low thousands. In mainstream settings the adoption of behaviourist intervention is understandably partial, with significant consequences. Faced with organisational complexity, any attempt to adopt a closed model of inclusion can only produce incongruity and exaggerate difficulties. To seek to address EBD from a standpoint of assumed objectivity is to put distance between ourselves and the 'problem pupil'. This may carry some short-term sense of comfort - the pupil's difficulties are nothing to do with teachers or other interested adults - but such denial can only be counter-productive, not least because the distance is illusory and it reduces the range of variables which can be manipulated to stimulate change.

For special schools the challenge is not dissimilar. For, while they may be better able to sustain a coherent model of response to individuals' EBD, this needs to be related to and moderated by consideration of the whole school dimension, including the behaviour of all pupils and staff and models of teaching and learning. A preoccupation with the features of a closed model, far from being less pernicious in special schools, may be more damaging, precisely because of the impression that controlled, individualistic approaches are sustainable. A special school which operates from this perspective is unlikely to engage in the progressive collaboration with the mainstream sector, as described in the Green Paper or *Programme of Action*.

At the risk of upsetting mathematicians, an understanding of the interaction between a pupil with EBD and others may be expressed as an equation $\Sigma\mathbf{b} = \mathbf{brc}$, where Σ is 'the impact of', $\mathbf{b}$ is a behaviour (in this case a pupil behaviour), $\mathbf{r}$ is the response to that behaviour and $\mathbf{c}$ is the context in which the interaction takes place. Whereas an exclusive concentration on $\mathbf{b}$ is inevitably restrictive - again, built around an expectation of the pupil becoming 'good' at the things they are not skilled at - the inclusion of $\mathbf{r}$ and $\mathbf{c}$ opens up (unlimited?) creative possibilities (variation in teacher's behaviour including language, classroom arrangements, curriculum content, teaching and learning styles, and so on). At least implicit in this validation of such diversity within an intervention strategy is the assertion that, in educational contexts, the creation of conditions which encourage and support change, is more effective than a direct effort to modify pupil behaviour. Indeed, where an assumption is made that we can change a pupil's behaviour directly, we are faced with a contradiction, on the one hand dismissing his/her defence that "someone made me do it", while on the other expecting him/her to respond to our attempts to effect behavioural change.

In his analysis of effective responses to EBD, Cole (1998) concludes that, at the teacher level,

'personal qualities of commitment, empathy and organisational skills are required of staff in abundance but

not mysterious and exclusive methods to teach and motivate pupils', (p114) while whole school factors which can compound or create difficulties include

> 'shortcomings on the organisation and ethos of school communities which...can neglect the needs of the less able, thereby precipitating alienation and difficult behaviour from those who feel they have little stake in the school'. (p115)

For intervention to be informed by this broader appreciation of the dynamics of EBD, there must be a meaningful commitment to both in-service training and school development. As far as the former is concerned, professional development should not be focused on consolidating the skills of a minority of specialist 'EBD teachers', as originally proposed by the Teacher Training Agency (TTA, 1998a, 1998b), but be a concern for all, as indicated in the general observations of the Elton Report (DfE, 1989). Echoing Elton, McLean (1992) is optimistic about the consequences of engaging all staff in ownership of the difficulties and the solutions:

> 'Energy and positive attitudes can replace exhaustion and disillusion only if a positive approach is adopted in which teachers perceive the management of pupils' behaviour as an issue about which everyone has something to learn and something to give'. (p30)

Here, the source of McLean's (1992) optimism is the suspension of traditional mainstream views that responsibility for intervention over EBD rests with a few key players within the school (SENCO and managers of the pastoral system), from outside the school (behaviour support teachers, educational psychologists and so forth) or wholly outside the school (special schools and units) and a similar stance must be adopted in order for the institutional response of schools to be as enlightened. To achieve the sort of effective response modelled within the University of Birmingham's recent research (Daniels et al, 1998), established orthodoxies need to be challenged. For example, even early intervention, which is almost universally hailed as an essential ingredient of successful responses, should be subject to a critical gaze, to ensure that it does not equate with early labelling and early preparation for social exclusion. Likewise, multi-agency practice, the rhetoric of which is compelling, but the practice of which can be superficial, undermined by unresolved territorial issues and consequently of little benefit to children and young people.

This critical rethinking of the stock assumptions of approaches to pupils with EBD is at least implicit in the Green Paper and *Programme of Action*, with their shift of emphasis towards the school level of response. On a broader front, it may also be detected within the contemporary, governmental drive towards greater social inclusion. However, if in the process, the interests of pupils with EBD remain largely subsumed in and marginalised by general policy considerations, there is every likelihood that interventions over pupils' EBD become less informed about the nature of those difficulties, less effective and less relevant to the needs of pupils.

Put another way, if the rhetoric of social inclusion translates into the practice of simply including greater numbers of people in social institutions without those institutions changing their shape, we will have no more inclusive a society than we have already. The real challenge of inclusion is to reshape social institutions to become more tolerant, flexible and accepting of diversity and less concerned with assimilation and normalisation. To make this a key focus of work with pupils with EBD is to open up the possibility that these pupils and our responses to them can become an invaluable source of insight and regeneration for the education service as a whole.

References

Clark, C., Dyson, A. and Milward, A. (1995) *Towards Inclusive Schools?*, London: David Fulton.

Cole, T. (1998) 'Understanding challenging behaviour' in Tilstone, C., Florian, L. and Rose, R. (eds) *Promoting Inclusive Practice*, London: Routledge.

Daniels, H., Visser, J., Cole, T. & de Reybekill, N. (1998) *Emotional and Behavioural Difficulties in Mainstream Schools (Research Report RR90)*, London: DfEE.

DES (1981) *The Education Act*, London: HMSO.

DfE (1989) *The Committee of Enquiry into Discipline in Schools in England and Wales (The Elton Report)*, London: HMSO.

DfE (1994a) *Code of Practice on the Identification and Assessment of Special Educational Needs*, London: HMSO.

DfE (1994b) *The Education of Children with Emotional and Behavioural Difficulties (Circular 9/94)*, London: HMSO.

DfEE (1997) *Excellence for all children: meeting Special Educational Needs (CM3785)*, London: The Stationery Office.

DfEE (1998a) *Meeting Special Educational Needs: A programme of action*, London: The Stationery Office.

DfEE (1998b) *Fair Funding: Improving Delegation to Schools*, London: The Stationery Office.

Forest, M. and Pearpoint, J. (1992) 'Putting All the Kids on the MAP', *Educational Leadership* 50(2): 26-31.

McLean, A. (1992) 'A Staff Development Approach to Improving Behaviour in Schools' in Lloyd, G. (ed) *Chosen to Care? - Responses to Disturbing and Disruptive Behaviour*, Edinburgh: Moray House.

Rouse, M. and Florian, L. (1996) 'Effective inclusive schools: a study in two countries', *Cambridge Journal of Education* 26(1): 71-85.

TTA (1998a) *National Standards for Special Educational Needs (SEN) Specialist Teachers* (Draft for Consultation), London: The Stationery Office.

TTA (1998b) *Options for the Delivery of Training for Special Educational Needs (SEN) Specialists* (Draft for Consultation), London: The Stationery Office.

Chapter Four

Ethical Practice:
key considerations when working with young people in difficulty

by Mark Provis

Troubled young people often act out their difficulties in ways that challenge organisations and their functioning.

The behaviour of this group of troubled young people triggers exceptional responses from teachers, schools and local education authorities. Increasingly these responses recognise that the most effective way of meeting the needs of such individuals is to support them within their own local context. Even so, some young people can be so challenging in their behaviour that there is some perceived need to segregate them or separate them out from others. Whenever their needs are met, it is important that the values system of mainstream society is upheld.

This values system is often taken to be implicit rather than made explicit. Practitioners who are drawn to working with troubled young people are likely to share both a common sense of purpose and some core values. It is important in providing consistency of adult care and concern that these values are made explicit and upheld by all practitioners in every context. Clearly articulating such values is not easy. Bentley (1998), in *Learning Beyond the Classroom,* argues that there is a cluster of values that informs our actions and activity. He states that:

> 'Even in secular, supposedly value–neutral systems, the liberal virtues of individual freedom, tolerance, mutual respect and fairness have been implicitly cherished.' (p3)

Bentley's view that there is a cluster of common values and qualities that we share is both helpful and hopeful. When he considers what the application of these values may mean he states,

> 'Motivating young people to take their place in the world with intelligence and consideration for others depends on allowing them to take responsibility for what they do.' (p7)

His thesis about the learning for all children seems to resonate especially well when considering our approach to working with troubled young people. He views the potential impact of teachers with considerable optimism.

> 'Schools can play a significant part in helping young people to know themselves and those around them, to recognise emotional risks and problems and to address them before they become chronic.' (p26)

Teachers are mandated to enable effective teaching and learning in their classrooms. Where their classrooms include young people with particular need, their responsibility extends to meeting that need and ensuring that it does not inhibit or prevent effective learning. Where this need is in the realm of emotional and behavioural difficulty, the teacher's role explicitly extends to working with the whole child to enable him/her to learn most effectively.

Bentley's view, built upon the work of Coleman (1996) on Emotional Intelligence and that of Salovey and Mayer (1990) states that:

> 'Even severe emotional problems and trauma can be tackled through emotional relearning. With time and careful support, children and young people can learn to reduce the effects of traumatic experience – of abuse, violence or neglect – by learning to recognise the source of their distress, rehearsing and revisiting the experience, and developing other, more positive components of their emotional portfolio.' (p25)

Teachers, in their work with young people experiencing such difficulties, have a critical role in supporting, enabling and reinforcing such emotional relearning.

As individual practitioners with troubled young people we bring our professional selves to the task and, because of the interpersonal nature of the task, we inevitably bring our social selves. There are times when the intensity of the intervention with young people can mean that our inner self may feel troubled or even threatened in turn. Haynes (1998) articulates the concept that at the core of ethical work is the development of a self that takes account of the relationship with others. She states:

> 'Ethics is about the construction of a self or person in relation to other social beings or persons.' (p149)

She explores the origin of this ethical self and questions whether there are visible, tangible principles i.e. things that can be clearly articulated, or whether they come together in a less overt and more subtle way.

She questions whether our ethical position develops from intuitive feelings and beliefs, particulars and principles, responsiveness and impartiality, clarity and simplicity about the right thing to do. Later, Haynes argues that our ethical position has been heavily influenced by past social practices. This much subtler, less explicit and developmental view of our ethical selves implies that making our separate and different ethical positions explicit is a challenging task.

Working collaboratively in the cause of providing effective teaching to aid enabling the learning of troubled young people requires us to make these ethical principles explicit and shared. This is necessary in ensuring young people are provided with appropriate care, consistency and consequences for their actions.

There is a pragmatic basis for such an approach. Through the clear development of a well-articulated ethical basis for our work, we can claim legitimacy for our actions. This becomes increasingly important where the basis for teacher authority is increasingly questioned. Robertson (1996) in his foreword to *Effective Classroom Control* expresses the view that the basis for teachers' long-term authority is:

> '...not simply the ascribed powers, institutional status and role, but more the personal qualities they possess which contribute to their effectiveness as teachers.' (pxi)

Robertson's view of the significance of the 'teacher self' for effective classroom management relates well with Haynes' concept of ethics being based upon the construction of a self in relation to other social beings or persons.

Working with troubled young people requires a degree of resilience and inner strength. However, if our ambition is limited to surviving them and/or simply controlling them, then we bring a very shrunken or limited ethical self to the task. Such an individual is likely to have friction-led and conflict-based relationships with the young people in question. They are likely to be constantly reinforced in their limited view of the potential of young people and to miss the opportunities to enable young people to learn and change through positive interaction with a concerned and competent adult.

A narrow pragmatic and limited professional self can start to take decisions from a position that Haynes describes as prudential rather than ethical. The framework for decision taking becomes confined and the question of generalisability and care for others becomes lost.

A real ethical test has to be whether a decision we are about to take bears scrutiny in other contexts and with other young people.

When working with troubled young people, the critical test of our ethical self probably becomes most tested when behaviour has broken down, relationships are at risk and the question of physical intervention comes into consideration. Young people who have been subject to emotional, physical or sexual abuse are much more likely to mistrust adults, to question their right to control and to dispute and challenge their authority. When faced with such a challenge it is important that those professionals working with troubled young people have a clear and well-developed ethical self for managing such interactions. Martin Herbert (1998), in describing an approach to working with young people and their families, posed a series of self questions from:

1. Why am I involved in this?
     through
2. Do I have the right to intervene?
     to
3. What is my system of support?

This self-questioning enables a values system and ethical position to be clearly stated. For class teachers, whose interaction with troubled young people is ongoing, some equally searching but different questions may apply.

Where we have had a confrontation with a young person we may wish to question:

1. Have I, the professional, conducted myself in a proper manner? In other words, if I am the competent, capable mature person in this interaction, have I conducted myself in a way that has shown:
     - a clear recognition of this individual's needs;
     - careful planning to meet this need;

- enthusiasm and commitment to enabling this young person to learn;
- understanding that this means planning for the learning of the 'whole young person';
- proper respect and regard for them as an individual?

In its most critical but elusive quality, the self question needs to be 'am I clear that I am not behaving in a way that mirrors/echoes the negative adult behaviour that first contributed to this young person's difficulties?'

The failure to do this-self check can mean that professionals inadvertently can 'become' the adult figure from the young person's past. The effect upon them may be to release their past anger at such adults and to enact it against this individual in the here and now. When this does occur, the target for such anger can be very shaken by the vigour of the attack and the level of rage expressed.

This does not suggest we avoid issues with young people or fail to enable them to face up to their difficulties. There is a need to reject unwanted or unacceptable behaviour but the basis for this has to be to further enable the young person's learning. The rejection needs to be of the unwanted behaviour whilst still communicating care and concern for the individual. Such an approach enables the young person to learn from their behaviour, to face up to its consequences and to change. The motive for doing so may rest upon the basis of preserving the relationship with this positive, committed enthusiastic adult figure.

The second and perhaps even more challenging self question is:

2.   Have I the right to intervene in such a direct and intrusive way?

This is the very difficult test of reasonableness. In this instance it is made more complex by context. If the group I am faced with is made up of 'ordinary young people' with no known exceptional difficulties, one level of interaction or intervention may seem legitimate. If I am working with a group where every member has known and explicitly acknowledged behaviour difficulties, are the expectations of reasonableness in my response any different? I would argue that the upholding of reasonableness of response becomes paramount in the second instance.

I may be unsettled and concerned at the challenge on my level of control. If that challenge may seem contagious, and others in the group may catch it, then I am likely to feel even more anxious. If I convey this anxiety through stiffening of posture, tightness of gesture or rising cadence of voice, I may signal to the individual and, perhaps, other volatile members of the group, that I am concerned that I may be losing authority and control. This in turn may accelerate the challenging interaction in the room. If I then target an individual and provide a vigorous reaction to their behaviour to secure control – I need to consider what has happened:

- Did I experience the initial challenge as personal?
- Did I convey any anxiety about this challenge to the group?
- Did the group/individuals within it react to my non-verbal cues and accentuate the challenge?
- Did I then react and target an individual to protect me and then perhaps beyond me the authority of the school?

Where interactions have gone awry and relationships have broken down and physical intervention has been deemed to be reasonable, such an ethical self-questioning review becomes unlikely. The professional body that we belong to provides us with support, the organisation that is the school, for which we act as an agent, reinforces and protects our position. Under such circumstances the likelihood of a serious and candid professional dialogue on the matter is much diminished. This is unfortunate, as the professional's opportunity for critical self-learning is lost.

Where such opportunities are repeatedly lost or ignored then we are faced by a serious question of risk. Staff learn that self-protective behaviour becomes the norm, such interventions become commonplace and the workplace becomes unusual and different from other mainstream settings. The climate and culture of the school entity becomes split and divided, with teachers and pupils lacking a common purpose, and the sense of an 'Us' and 'Them' environment gets reinforced again and again.

Where the momentum outlined above starts to develop, it becomes self-sealing. Inspection or review of the organisation's formal systems may fail to reveal any difficulties. It is possible for a self-sealing organisation to have:

- a clear behaviour policy for pupils;
- a practice guide for staff;

- communications of behavioural expectations to all parents;
- rigorous record keeping of all 'incidents'.

It is in the softer processes of the school and in the signals and signs of its culture that the real ethical practice is defined. The ethical commitment of the staff is expressed in what they say and do and how they say it and do it. It is in these softer more elusive aspects of practice that our ethical commitment can be measured. The evidence for this is provided by examples of staff exploring the third critical self question.

Do I have the necessary skills to undertake this intervention? The question is not simply a moment in time issue. It is one that needs to be returned to again and again. Where the response is 'no' or one of uncertainty then the onus is upon me to clearly state this and to seek support in securing such skills. It needs to be recognised that this is far from easy in a negative self-sealing environment. Where the question is put in such environments, it can challenge the culture and effect change. Equally, it may be rejected and the individual who put the question may feel let down or even 'scapegoated' by the organisation. However, there can be little doubt as to which forms the ethical act.

Even where the answer is 'yes', the question does not stop there. As an ethical practitioner, keen to provide the 'best professional self' for troubled young people, I need to face up to two further questions.

Do I share these skills with colleagues in dialogue, in supervision and through ongoing development events? There needs to be recognition that self skills development is an ethical requisite but we should not be doing this selfishly and that there is a team/community of colleagues with whom we should pool our skills - not least to provide the consistency of care and response that troubled young people most need.

There is a further dimension which has to be:

3.   Do I continue to develop and refine my skills?

This remains so important throughout our professional careers. The societal context in which we practise is constantly developing. We have an obligation to be responsive to this and to adapt and grow in response to these demands. This becomes even more challenging in mid or late career when it is the brave and ethically committed professionals who continue to be able to say – I still need to learn more.

Victoria Neumark (1998) in her article commenting on the DfEE guidance to teachers on the use of force, drew out a critical difference in teachers as opposed to wider society's use of force. She states that police officers deal with incidents and then walk away. Teachers, by contrast, have an ongoing relationship within the young people in the classroom and need to consider the consequences of their actions and the effect of these actions on continuing relationships. She properly reflects that force should only be used as a last resort. To ensure that force is rarely considered as a response, there needs to be a premium placed upon positive teaching and the development of wide-ranging skills to prevent and manage incidents with young people effectively. These considerations are of even greater relevance to those professionals who work with troubled young people.

Working ethically requires continuous discussion with colleagues, constant reflection upon practice and a commitment to continuous learning. Even then complex dynamic interactions are difficult situations to manage. Bentley comments:

> 'living ethically often requires us to make decisions between different kinds of good'. (p61)

This is especially true of working with groups of troubled young people. Such work is complex, challenging and yet very rewarding. Simplistic, specific, rigid guidelines will rarely serve as a realistic ethical framework. We are often faced with the dilemma of:

upholding rules	v	developing norms
applying power	v	exercising authority
protecting self	v	protecting others
securing control	v	enabling freedom

The case outlined above argues that the mature, ethical professional is constantly striving to be on the right hand side of these dilemmas whenever possible. Professionals working with troubled young people are often engaged with the very learning group that Bentley says society has 'dumped' - the young people whom the public agencies have marginalised or for whom they have ceased to exercise full responsibility. Ethical professional commitment requires us to restore mainstream expectations through our relationship building, reinforced by our professional practice, to enable troubled young people to resolve their difficulties. This commitment holds true in work with troubled young people across mainstream and marginalised settings.

A pivotal moment in the life of a troubled young person is often the point at which a professionally led intervention begins. It is not good enough that such an intervention is well-meaning or well-intended. It is inadequate if it is pivotally based upon the utilitarian principle of being in the interest of or for the good of others. All professionals engaged in such an intervention need to be working from a platform of well-informed expertise. Their intervention needs to be grounded in a positive plan for change, that brings together all of the resources around a troubled young person into a framework of efficient and effective support for them.

If this is the task, then it makes greater demands upon the ethical social self that I bring to the work. Not only do I need to make my values explicit, but I need to share them with all of the adults involved to secure clarity of purpose and consistency for the young person. Moreover, I need to understand the values system and ethical practice of the other professionals involved in order to secure optimum outcomes for the young person. As part of our ethical practice, teachers need to learn to work effectively with social workers, probation officers, youth workers, health professionals and youth offending team practitioners to obtain the best outcome for an intervention. Often the failure to do so means that:
- opportunities are lost
- critical moments of change are missed
- resources are wasted

and the professionals become a part of the young person's problems rather than the catalyst for solutions.

References

A.M.M.A. (1995) *The Checklist for Children, Local Authorities and the UN Convention on the rights of the child,* London: A.M.M.A.
Bentley, T. (1998) *Learning Beyond the Classroom Demos,* London: Routledge.
Coleman, D. (1996) *Emotional Intelligence. Why it can matter more than IQ,* London: Bloomsbury.
Haynes, F. (1998) *The Ethical School,* London: Routledge.
Herbert, M. (1998) *Working with children and their families,* London: Routledge.
Neumark, V. (1998) Force Factor, *Times Educational Supplement* 11 September, 1999.
Robertson, J. (1996) *Effective Classroom Control,* London: Hodder & Stoughton.
Salovey, P. and Mayer, J.D. (1990) *Emotional Intelligence, Imagination, Cognition & Personality* 9, 185 - 211.

Chapter Five

The 'Matching Process':
key factors influencing pupil behaviour in school

by Richard Stakes

The importance of matching the expectations made of children at home with the demands of school is regarded as a crucial part of determining scholastic success, as well as affecting the self-confidence and self-esteem of pupils (e.g. Warnock, 1978; Widlake & McCloud, 1984; Wolfendale, 1992; Bastiani & Wolfendale, 1996). Through the presentation of some recent research evidence, and reference to traditional perspectives describing emotional and behavioural difficulties (EBD), as well as the educational context represented by the classroom and the National Curriculum, this chapter will firstly argue for the importance of an understanding of this matching process. It will concentrate particularly on two crucial aspects of this process: behavioural management and curriculum differentiation. Secondly, this chapter will discuss some of the recent initiatives and research evidence concerned with helping children with behavioural difficulties, their parents and teachers towards alleviating these problems.

Behaviour and learning difficulties in the school context

Martin and Hayes (1998) pointed out that until relatively recently it is the child who has largely been the focus of attention when discussing behavioural issues. In their view, it is the child who is seen as having the problem or having difficulties. Further, it is the case that traditionally children with EBD were identified within a medical model that is generally deficit-based, and which focused upon their personal inabilities and deficiencies.

Greenhalgh (1994) pointed out that those children identified as having EBD were in fact a subset of a wider description of behavioural difficulties, and commonly regarded as suffering from an illness. In the medical model, it is the nature of the child that is regarded as a key focus of attention when dealing with children's behaviour.

However, McMannus (1989), whilst acknowledging the importance of understanding the nature of the child, argued that this was not the only feature that needed to be taken into account when discussing behaviour. He argued that children's background nurturing is of equal importance in determining influences on behaviour.

Molnar and Lindquist (1989), Farrell (1995) and McNamara and Moreton (1995) have all put the case equally strongly, arguing that a child's behavioural difficulties must be seen in the wider environmental context of their social, cultural and racial circumstances. Both Farrell (1995) and McNamara and Moreton (1995) asserted that the medical model of dealing with unacceptable behaviour in school is both simplistic and inappropriate. The approach to behavioural analysis, espoused by the environmental school of thought, taking into account the family circumstances within the social and cultural milieu of the school, is commonly described as the ecosystemic perspective. This approach encompasses all of the interactions (both positive and negative) between a child and their total environment to account for their behaviour.

With the ecosystemic perspective in mind, Greenhalgh (1994) proposed that theories of transactional analysis could make a valuable contribution to our understanding of behaviour. He reasoned that the transactional model indicates how behaviour is dependent on learned 'scripts' or particular roles that we internalise and use to live out in our daily lives. These roles are, in Greenhalgh's view, based on personal constructs that are influenced by our position within the dynamics of our family.

Further, Greenhalgh (1994) pointed out that the social and emotional experiences of children are neither consistent, nor static. Rather, a child's experiences can be open to widely different behavioural expectations in different social contexts. It is as part of this developing process that children are expected to match their behaviour to the many different social situations to which they are exposed. For example, when at home, children have to match the behavioural and social expectations set within the norms and values of their family. Similarly, in school they have to meet these expectations within the norms set by their teachers and the institutional values and mores determined by the school.

It is not necessarily the case that the values and expectations of the home and the school will coincide, rather it is often that these can be quite different, leading to misunderstandings and tensions for all concerned.

Nevertheless, within this complex web of social interaction, most children manage to cope and even to prosper. Some children, however, and particularly those with EBD, appear to experience greater difficulties in matching these values, attitudes and expectations. In some cases children can run into serious difficulties in school, becoming disruptive and disaffected.

School exclusions

Serious disruption and disaffection can lead to the imposition of sanctions on pupils. Commonly there is a hierarchy of sanctions available within school; the most serious of which is exclusion. Three types of exclusions were formulated in the *1986 Education Act*. These were described as fixed term, indefinite and permanent exclusions.

Figures from the DfEE (1997) provide evidence that in recent years there has been a massive increase in the numbers of children who are being excluded from attending school. In 1991 official figures showed that the number of permanent exclusions from school was 2,190, by 1996 this figure had risen to 12,476 (DfEE, 1997). The figures also show that the biggest number of exclusions were in the secondary phase of schooling: 1,608 children were excluded from primary schools and 524 from special school, while the figure for secondary schools was 10,344. This evidence also tells us that the age range of pupils is extending to include those at Key Stage 1.

A breakdown of the figures supplied by the DfEE (1997) indicated further that there is a tendency for some more than other groups of children to be excluded. The figures show, for example, that boys were more likely to be excluded than girls, Afro-Caribbean children were four times more likely to be excluded than other children and 17% of children excluded had a Statement of Special Educational Needs.

Explicit reasons for the large rise in school exclusions and suspensions are difficult to ascertain; nevertheless, a wide range of possible reasons has been suggested for this dramatic increase in number. An analysis shows that these reasons cover both general and specific causes. General explanations include unacceptable and uncooperative behaviour (Parsons & Howlett, 1996; DfE, 1994) and a lack of respect for school and teachers. Specific causes that have been cited include: the introduction of the National Curriculum programme (Stakes & Hornby, 1996), less tolerance on the part of teachers (Blandford, 1996), changes in attitude as a result of the increased assessment base of education, the publication of results and performance tables, (Parsons and Howlett, 1996), a lack of appropriate resources, as well as the effect of wider parental choice (Williamson, 1998).

The tendency to exclude pupils with problem behaviour has clearly increased in mainstream schools. The extent to which this is an effective or efficient provision for pupils deemed inappropriately placed is questionable. So too, perhaps, is the psychological or educational reasoning which might be applied to operating this kind of system. What is required, arguably, is a more clearly established reference point in theory as well as a shared thinking in shaping up responses and provision for pupils showing undesirable behaviour.

Undesirable behaviour

Evidence collected in recent years has indicated a less than positive picture of children's experience of school. A report in *The Guardian* (1996) suggested that some 50% of pupils in secondary schools were bored by their experience there. More seriously, another report by the children's charity Childline (1996), showed that in a study of one thousand children in 16% secondary schools, 79% of them were more worried about examinations and schoolwork than anything else in their lives. This survey also revealed that 66% of those pupils asked were also worried about their future. In another group of 200 pupils questioned, 13 had contemplated suicide, while one had attempted it. In terms of well-being, confidence and 'satisfaction', young people at school seem more rather than less at risk emotionally than they were previously.

Poor behaviour is not just a school-based problem. There is also evidence of parental concerns. An ICM/LWT survey (1993) found that many parents lacked confidence when managing and disciplining their children. In particular, this survey revealed more than one-quarter of parents in Britain believed their children were out of control; one-third found disciplining their children a problem; one in five were unable to cope with their children's lying; and 44% of children disobeyed their parents about bedtime.

Research evidence also indicates that there are discrepancies between children's behaviour that concern teachers within the classroom and that which concerns their parents. As far as teachers are concerned, evidence collected over many years (for example Wickman, 1928; Wragg & Dooley, 1984; DES, 1989) indicated that views about undesirable behaviour not only remain relatively constant but were also focused more or less exclusively on what can be described as relatively minor problems. The Elton Report (DES, 1989), for example, found that it was the frequency of the occurrence of certain behaviours with which teachers found coping the most difficult. This research showed that most commonly cited behaviours concerning teachers included excessive noise, not paying attention, being 'off task', talking out of turn, lying and physical aggression towards others, unsolicited wandering around the classroom and general disobedience.

Moore (1966) in his work with parents produced a significantly different list of difficulties reported by their children. This list, beyond the general reluctance to attend school, cited children reporting difficulties in relationships with their teachers, their peers, taking school dinners and using school toilets. This evidence when compared with that reported by teachers indicates that the difficulties encountered have quite different perspectives from both parties involved. Secondly, it is interesting to note that both teachers and parents were apparently more concerned with social and interactional, than with psychological or educational explanations for undesirable behaviour.

Matching home-school expectation and acceptable behaviour
As indicated earlier, Greenhalgh (1994) argued that behaviour is closely linked to individual values taken from within personal constructs that relate to what is regarded as acceptable and unacceptable conduct. These constructs are individual and can be widely different in different situations. What is acceptable conduct in a child's home may not match that in another where he or she is a visitor. Similarly, membership of one community may not prepare a child for acceptance in another community. As far as the child is concerned they have to learn that the routines, social conventions and the form that acceptable behaviour takes can vary widely in different social circumstances.

Realising this can sometimes be a confusing and complex process. This form of learning perhaps can best be described as a matching process for the child. It is the child who individually has to match their understanding and experiences to individual situations. They need to match the acceptable behaviour of their home with that regarded as acceptable within the classroom and then with both of these situations to that of the school playground. As they grow older, the same children may have to match the accepted behaviour in such diverse social circumstances as the Saturday afternoon football crowd with that expected of a church congregation the following day.

The language used to define what is acceptable behaviour often can be a crucial determinant of a child's expectations within social situations. From an adult's point of view, they may feel that their language is clear, while from the child's perspective this may not be the case. Such phrases as 'toeing the line' or 'meeting the mark' may, in real terms, be meaningless to a child. For example: what line? or what mark? Further, even when they have some concept of the meaning of such phrases, this mark or line will, more than likely, be both figurative and variable, as it is mentally drawn by different adults to represent their own viewpoint. Such uncertainty can often leave the child or young person confused as to the behaviour that is expected of them in different social circumstances.

With the relationship between the home and the school in mind, it is the case that teachers and pupils approach the matching problem from very different perspectives. From the child or young person's point of view, the key is an understanding of their personal relationship between the values and expectations set within their family and those espoused by the school. As far as teachers are concerned, their main focus of acceptable behaviour in the classroom is possibly pragmatic - control and order. Their priorities are set not only around the requirement to accommodate the needs of an individual child, or perhaps a relatively small group of children. Rather, the teachers' concern generally focuses on the management and accommodation of a large group of children who, depending on their home circumstances, may hold widely differing views on what is acceptable behaviour.

Donaldson (1978) pointed out that for some children the range of attitudes and actions describing acceptable behaviour within the home can be very different from those encountered within the school. In such circumstances, she argues, the child has to be able to not only understand there are differences in expectation in the different social situations but also to select the appropriate behaviour. Further she claims this may provide young children, particularly those with perceptual difficulties, with difficulties about what is expected of them within the school setting.

For many children the relationship between the expectations laid down at home and those at school, although having an element of adjustment of their understanding and actions, appears not to be a major problem. They appear to be able to cope with the differences when they occur without too many problems. For some children the adjustments that are necessary are seemingly much more difficult, even traumatic. It is not clear what makes the difference. However, a number of features have been cited as contributory factors. These include the effect of personal constructs on a child's understanding of different behavioural expectations in different social situations (Greenhalgh, 1994); their ability to internalise what they have already learned, their level of trust of adults, the influence of the model of self-fulfilling prophecies, and their level of personal resilience.

For those children who find the home-school transition difficult and whose personal resilience is not strong, this adjustment can be fraught, even traumatic. Such difficulties can lead to confusion and frustration, resulting not only in inappropriate behaviour in school but also poor academic performance. It is, more often than not, these children who tax the skills and professional resilience of their teachers and for whom teachers have to show the most flexibility and resourcefulness to accommodate their behaviour.

Where there are difficulties, the onus is on the skill of the teacher and their ability to link their own expectations with those of the individual child. This calls for a professional flexibility of approach. This approach must take into account the behaviour of those children that falls outside the boundaries of acceptability within the classroom and that of those children who show inconsistent behaviour that swings between what is and is not acceptable within the social confines of the classroom. Such inconsistencies of behaviour can evolve from a range of sources, from relationships within the school and outside it, as well as their level of motivation and enthusiasm. It is an important truism that good classroom practice will reduce the chances of difficulties becoming disruptions for those children who are most at risk.

The National Curriculum
The issue of matching is not only relevant to behavioural management, it is also vitally important within the context of the National Curriculum. The underpinning philosophy of the National Curriculum was that it should be a *broad and balanced* programme to *promote the spiritual,*

moral, cultural, mental and physical development of all pupils throughout the period of compulsory schooling as a preparation for adult life (NCC, 1989:1). This is a programme that has not been introduced without some controversy over its value for all children in school, particularly those with SEN.

The evidence collected about the value of the National Curriculum with children with SEN has produced some mixed results. Ashdown, for example, writing in the *British Journal of Special Education* commented:

> 'The introduction of the National Curriculum in England and Wales in 1988 created special problems because it was not formulated with children with SEN in mind.'
>
> (Ashdown, 1994: 110)

Reiser commented similarly, describing National Curriculum provision as:

> '...too prescriptive, even irrelevant in the case of children with severe learning difficulties.'
>
> (Reiser, 1994: 2)

In Reiser's view, even the 1995 revision of the National Curriculum had not met all the concerns of teachers.

The need for the curriculum to be relevant for children has been long acknowledged. Teachers of children with SEN are often particularly well aware of the need to develop their professional skills in matching (differentiating) their teaching materials to the level of ability of their children as well as the pace at which they can successfully deal with it.

The need to differentiate materials for specific children with the requirements of the National Curriculum programme has created its own problems. Norwich (1993) argued that the National Curriculum programme is a *'form of tokenism'* and is *'inappropriate'* for providing experiential learning for many children with SEN. Norwich called for an alternative approach, emphasising mastery and a sense of achievement for the pupil with SEN. The first approach, in his view, would lead only to confusions and anxieties for both pupils and teachers.

For Williamson too, new developments were received less than favourably. The introduction of formal testing as part of the National Curriculum programme was described as quite simply *catastrophic for the minority - the 20% of young people who were not achieving academically* (Williamson, 1998:p113). The question has also been raised as to the effectiveness of the National Curriculum in raising academic standards for all children. Williamson (1998), for example, commenting in the spread of GCSE results in 1997, points out that although standards had been raised for the majority of children, the process had widened the gap between the most successful pupils and their least successful counterparts. This point was reinforced by the GCSE results in 1998.

Ball (1998) also contributed to this debate about the implications of educational reform and made the point that the further widening of parental choice over schools and the introduction of league tables of school test and examination results encouraged schools to exclude more children. The children most 'at risk' from these reforms are, she argues, those that schools find the most difficult to control, motivate, and least likely to gain good examination results.

As far as teachers of children with EBD are concerned, an analysis of their views on the value of the National Curriculum falls similarly into two discrete categories: negative and positive. The overall negative point of view is perhaps best exemplified by Orr (1995) who described the effect of the National Curriculum as 'a prescription for failure.' Similar, more particular criticisms of the programme have been raised by Cooper, Smith and Upton (1994), Peagram (1995), Marchant (1995) and Upton (1996).

However, some of the evidence collected about the value of the National Curriculum programme for children with EBD is more positive. Research by Davies and Landman (1991) indicated that a clear majority of teachers of children with EBD supported the introduction of the National Curriculum. They found that the teachers at this time were largely concerned with the enhancement of their own skills and the availability of resources to deliver certain parts of it.

Research conducted by Cole and Visser (1998) indicated that teachers working in EBD schools showed considerable support for both the principles and practice of the National Curriculum, less than half of those questioned supporting it without any real reservation. In a detailed investigation of teachers' views, this survey found that about half of those who were questioned felt that the introduction of the National Curriculum had enhanced their ability to manage children with EBD. A similar number reported they felt its introduction had helped to improve the academic achievement of their pupils. A further positive finding was that teachers reported that some pupils with EBD felt that the curriculum they were receiving was the same as their mainstream peers.

The survey by Cole, Visser and Upton (1998) also noted that teachers of children with EBD found the requirements of some National Curriculum subject areas easier to meet than other areas of the curriculum. Their evidence indicated that subject area requirements that teachers questioned felt were most easily covered across all the key stages were art, English and maths and PE. Similarly, the teachers reported that art and craft, PE and English were regarded as having the greatest 'therapeutic' value for their pupils, and that their pupils responded most favourably to art, English and design technology.

A way forward - the matching process
In the light of the evidence detailed above, relating to the difficulties that children with EBD have in matching the attitudes and aspirations of their home and school, it is important to look at recent research evidence that focuses on helping and promoting strategies to alleviate some of these problems. This section will consider these strategies under three headings: developing positive relationships between the home and the school, innovations that are being developed within the school and developments in behavioural management.

Developing home-school relationships
The importance of parent-teacher co-operation cannot be over-estimated in helping children towards an understanding of acceptable behaviour in school. This link is not only just a question of the development of a pupil's social compliance but also, as indicated earlier, is supported by a wide range of research as well as official reports. In short this link impacts upon a pupil's level of success in school. At an official level the Plowden Report (DES, 1967), for example, described the importance of the link between the education of the whole person and the family. Similarly, the Elton Report (DES, 1989) expressed the view that the most effective junior schools were those that had the best informal relationships with parents. Such convictions have since been consistently advocated (e.g. City of Leicester, 1932; Underwood, 1995; The Elton Report, DES, 1989).

In her research, Ball (1998) provided evidence of some recent collaborative programmes between parents and schools in the UK, which have contributed to improving the home-school relationship. In a number of the cases cited by Ball (1998), projects have not only improved school attendance and produced an increase in personal self-esteem but have also reduced local crime statistics among those children who have participated.

Some authorities have an established resource to support such a relationship. One in Hackney (Hancock, 1997), for example, has a threefold focus. These include projects for children such as home-school reading and maths (where parents and teachers collaborate to help), projects for children and parents together and projects for parents alone (where they can learn parenting skills and participate in a range of other learning activities.) Some encouraging reports are beginning to emerge from some of these projects. Other evidence from a recent comparative study in Haringey, reported by Ball (1998), indicated that where parents were involved in improving their child's reading, the greatest progress resulted.

However, despite these promising examples, questions have been raised about the ability of parents and teachers to collaborate together in such circumstances (for example: Hancock, 1997; Woodhead, 1997). Hancock, the co-ordinator of the Hackney Parents, Children and Teachers (PACT) group, noted that the parents and teachers do not always work together with ease. He argued there were three common difficulties: a tendency for teachers to be over-defensive when challenged or criticised by parents, an inclination by them to dominate in meetings with parents, and a lack of skills and experience in interacting with parents. Woodhead questioned the extent to which teachers have entered into meaningful partnerships with parents. He is cited by Ball (1998) as stating that 'teachers' working conditions allow little prime time for unhurried contact with parents' (p15).

Smith (1987) argued that one way forward is through the use of more comprehensive support being provided for parents and children by 'family centres', a label used for varied provision, which when fully realised has the following characteristics:

- commitment to work with both parents and children;
- a range of services for both children and adults;

- flexible working styles to suit the needs of families and individuals;
- a neighbourhood base from which most users are drawn;
- an emphasis on local involvement and participation by users;
- a community work or preventative approach;
- building on strengths and skills in the community rather than delivering services;
- aiming to increase the confidence and self-respect of users and to increase their skills and understanding of children.

Ball (1998) reported that staff in some family centres have been approached by local primary schools for help in coping with difficult behaviour in the classroom and in involving parents in their child's learning. The aim of empowering parents means that the family centre approach focuses on what parents can share with staff. Such an approach will need time to build relationships based on mutual trust to ensure this can happen.

There are, however, inherent difficulties with this approach. Firstly, there is not enough time in most primary schools to facilitate this type of activity. In addition, the empowerment approach requires sophisticated facilitating skills, which are not part of the primary teacher's training or experience. Ball (1998) also pointed out that one worker who visited a school to help teachers with 'classroom control' found herself left with the disruptive classes, providing respite but not much professional development for the teacher.

Other research has also provided examples of preschool-home links. Ball (1998) cited a number of examples from practice in the USA, which are being piloted in the UK. The basis of these links is educating parents to explore the practicalities of child rearing and to provide counselling and advice for parents of young children. One project is described as teaching parents a set of principles and skills about praise and play, how to set limits, how to deal with misbehaviour without harshness and how to develop communication and problem solving with families.

In a further example, Arnold (1995) provided details of one support group where participating children were provided with a 'child learning record'. This record contained details of activities, progress and advice, which aimed to give the family a sense of progress and achievement. In this project the work of the support programme deliberately overlapped with an after-school story club. This is a once-a-term activity of about 40 minutes, which is open to all Reception and Year 1 children, teachers and parents. These sessions have a number of activities. They offer an activity to children who are over the age for involvement in the project, give parents a chance to participate and reinforce the links between the preschool project and the school staff.

There is, however, a need for more information about the sources of support required by children in the middle childhood age-group (8-13). There is some evidence of regression in learning after transfer to secondary school and truancy and other 'at risk' behaviour is often rooted in the transition period. Research reported by Ball from the USA suggested that help at this age is:

> 'most effective when part of a network that includes peers, pets, parents, hobbies, and environmental sources of support'.

> (Ball, 1998: p22)

Ball (1998) also reported that unstructured opportunities to get away by oneself can help children to develop their social perspective and that organisations that allow children to experience autonomy and to master the content of an activity are most appropriate and work better than formal organisations and structured activities. Children in this age group need to be listened to and empathised with as well as having a regard to their perspective.

Innovation within school

Difficulties for some pupils in meeting the requirements laid out in the National Curriculum have also been identified as part of the reason for undesirable behaviour and are being addressed. David Blunkett, the Minister of Education (TES, 1998), justified such a move on the grounds that for disaffected teenagers something more than the National Curriculum should be offered. Recent Government initiatives such as the introduction of a greater flexibility to set aside up to two curriculum subjects at Key Stage 4 from science, design technology or a modern foreign language, have provided a greater curriculum flexibility for this age group. This relaxation of statute allows disaffected older pupils to spend up to one day a week on a Work-Related Learning scheme or continue their education in a further education college instead of school in an attempt to re-engage them in their education.

Circular 10/99, *Social Inclusion: Pupil Support* (DfEE, 1999) pointed out that there is no explicit legal requirement to teach a National Curriculum subject for any particular proportion of the curriculum time or, for that matter, any particular period of time. Furthermore, the same document emphasised the importance of modifying the National Curriculum for some pupils. It stated that to meet the needs of pupils, material from an earlier or later key stage than the notional key stage of the pupil may be appropriate. Beyond this, it indicated that schools are required to teach the programme of study for each key stage only by the end of that stage. Thus teachers will be given a degree of flexibility to enable better matching of individual difference to the curriculum, thereby tailoring a programme of study to a pupil's abilities, without them having to achieve the same standard as their peers.

The Draft Guidelines (1999, para. 4.37-40) also proposed changes to the procedure for temporary disapplication or modification of the National Curriculum for some pupils. Although the time allowed for a child to be disapplied from the National Curriculum will not be changed, that is, from up to six months in the first instance, it is proposed to allow a head teacher, in conjunction with others such as the child's parents, teachers and other relevant professionals, at the end of this period to be able to use his or her discretion to make provisional plans for a further period of disapplication. It is also stated that such an approach will enable the process of disapplication more simple to operate.

Leading the way, in terms of making greater use of this curriculum flexibility, are a number of the City Technology Colleges (CTCs). The CTCs have found that some of their pupils were best served by not rigorously following the requirements laid down by the National Curriculum. More recently state schools have looked for more flexibility within this framework. It is arguable that this can help them better serve the needs of children where greater differentiation of response has been shown to be important.

Resilience

Factors affecting the way schools respond more or less effectively to children with SEN are complex and many, but one such factor which has attracted increasing interest to researchers attempting to explain the difference in school contexts is the idea of resilience. Wang and Haertel (1999) argued that some more than other children with a background of social difficulties appear to be much more resilient to the stresses within school. In a summary of some recent research findings, Wang and Haertel (1999) argued that more effective provision for pupils with SEN can be achieved by improving levels of resilience in the individual. This is likely to occur when the following features can be found in the school context:

- there is strong commitment to the tasks that the children are given, when these tasks are personally challenging to them and are set in an appropriate cultural and motivational context;
- teachers are sensitive to the children's needs and to their prior achievements and when the children are given a responsibility for their own learning;
- teachers are both the transmitters of knowledge and the facilitators of learning;
- there is external support for children through teachers, learning support assistants and other appropriate resources in the classroom that take into account the level of children's ability and the pace of their learning;
- there are high expectations of children in a supportive environment;
- there are strong, positive links between the home and the school, allowing parents to take a key position in their own children's educational progress.

Building resilience is no easy option, and clearly sets out an educational intervention as fundamental to increasing life opportunities for young people and children who have, in terms of educational risk, been deemed disenfranchised or disadvantaged.

Behaviour Management

Initiatives to help schools develop a policy to meet the requirements of the *Education Act 1997* and to improve the standard of behaviour of pupils are growing. Kingston upon Hull, as part of an initiative to meet the requirements of the *Education Act 1997*, has produced a city wide discipline policy for use throughout its primary schools.

The 1997 Act, which can be interpreted as reflection of the political concern about school exclusions, triggered, in the case of Hull, what was an early attempt by a local authority to produce a national policy on school discipline. This was reinforced by the statutory requirement to produce Behaviour Support Plans as laid out in the Act. The Hull LEA involved teachers and governors in order to produce a disciplinary policy that would serve two purposes: to show children what was expected of them and to produce a consistency of approach throughout their primary schools.

Conclusion

This chapter has briefly outlined some of the difficulties in the complex, intricate and sometimes perplexing relationship between the home and the school. It has concentrated on the process of matching expectations in two areas in particular, home-school expectations and curriculum content. Despite recent research evidence it is clear that as far as the matching of expectations between home and school, there are no easy answers to overcoming the problems that these often conflicting areas represent. The evidence makes it clear that the only real way forward is through negotiation and developing mutual confidence and trust between children, their parents and their teachers.

The demands on teachers have changed over the years. The requirements of the National Curriculum leave teachers with little time or energy to do anything else. The National Curriculum now expects that 20% of the time in school will be spent on non-National Curricular activities. It is possible that this and other initiatives discussed above may help to more easily satisfy the need to match the curriculum presented to children with their own interests and skills. For teachers of children with EBD this may provide a flexibility that will allow more time to be spent on vocational or personal development work.

The solution may lie, at least in part, in offering what Ball (1998) has called 'a home within the school approach' to expertise from outside it. The need for planning is paramount to organise and deliver such an approach as well as evaluating its effectiveness. The success of this approach will surely rest on striking the match between home and school for many of the young people most at risk of educational breakdown.

Beyond this, the evidence shows that teachers need further training in working with parents as partners. Initial teacher training provides the minimum of help for teachers in training for working with children with EBD. These are both areas of work that should be given attention, with sound professional help being provided, and aimed at helping to alleviate some of the difficulties that arise in the complex triangle of relationships between children in school, their parents and the school.

References

Arnold, R. (1995) *The Improvement of Schools through Partnership; School, LEA and University.* Slough: NFER.

Ashdown, R. (1994) 'Planning for their Future.' *British Journal of Special Education,* 21, 3, 110-112.

Ball, M. (1998) *School Inclusion. The school, the family, the community.* York: Joseph Rowntree Trust.

Bastiani, J. and Wolfendale, S. (1996) (Eds) *Home-School Work in Britain. Review, Reflection and Development.* London: David Fulton.

Blandford, S. (1996) *Managing Discipline in Schools.* London: Routledge.

Buchanan, J. (1996) Presentation at the Launch of the Cambridge Youth Action Scheme.

Byers, (1994) The Dearing Review of the National Curriculum. *British Journal of Special Education.* 21, 3, 92-96.

Chapman, C. and Stone, J. (1996) in G. Upton. and V. Varma. (Eds) *Stress in SEN Teachers.* Aldershot: Arena.

Childline (1996) *Stressed Out.* London: Childline.

City of Leicester (1932) *Annual Report.* Leicester: Leicester City Council.

Cole, T. and Visser, J. (1998) 'How should the effectiveness of pupils with EBD be assessed?' *Emotional and Behavioural Difficulties,* 3, 1, 37-43.

Cole, T., Visser, J. and Upton G. (1998) *Effective Schooling for Pupils with Emotional and Behavioural Difficulties.* London: David Fulton.

Cooper, P., Smith, C. and Upton, G. (1994) *Emotional and Behavioural Difficulties.* London: Routledge.

Daniels, H. and Ware, J. (1991) (Eds) *Special Educational Needs and the National Curriculum, Impact of the Educational Reform Act.* London: Kogan Page Bedford Way Series.

Davies, J. D. and Landman, M. (1991) 'The National Curriculum in Special Schools for pupils with EBDs. A national survey.' *Maladjustment and Therapeutic Education,* 9, 3, 130-135.

DfE. (1994) Elton Report (1989) *Discipline in Schools.* London: HMSO.

DfE. (1994) *Code of Practice on the Identification and Assessment of Pupils with Special Educational Needs.* London: HMSO.

DfEE. (1997) *Permanent Exclusions from School in England (press notice).* No. 30, xi.

DfEE. (1999) Circular 10/99 *Social Inclusion: Pupil Support.* London: HMSO.

Department of Education and Science. (1989) *Discipline in Schools, The Elton Report.* London: HMSO.

Donaldson, M. (1978) *Children's Minds.* London: Fontana.

Farrell, P. (1995) *Children with Emotional and Behavioural Difficulties.* London: The Falmer Press.

Galton, M. (1998) *Inside the Primary School Classroom: 20 years on.* London: Routledge.

Graham, D. and Tyler, D. (1993) *A lesson for us all. The making of the National Curriculum.* London: Routledge.

Greenhalgh, P. (1994) *Emotional Growth and Learning*. London: Routledge.

Guardian (The) Taken from a report, 12 August 1996.

Hancock, R. (1997) We need to support a fragile movement. *Parenting Forum Newsletter.*

Horton, T. (1991) *Assessment Debates.* London: Routledge.

Hurt, P. H., and Peters, R. S. (1967) *The Logic of Education.* London: Routledge and Kogan Paul.

ICM/LWT survey reported in *The Sunday Times* 29 viii 1993.

Kyriacou, C. (1991) *Essential Teaching Skills.* Oxford: Blackwell.

Lewis, A. (1991) *Primary Special Needs and the National Curriculum.* London: Routledge.

Marchant, S. (1995) 'The essential curriculum for pupils exhibiting emotional and behavioural difficulties.' *Therapeutic Care and Education,* 4, 1, 36-47 .

Martin, H., and Hayes, S. (1998) 'Overcoming Obstacles: approaches to dealing with problem pupils.' *British Journal of Special Education,* 25, 3,135-139.

McMannus, M. (1989) *Troublesome behaviour in the classroom. A teachers' survival guide.* London: Routledge.

McNamara, S. and Moreton, G. (1995) *Changing Behaviour. Teaching Children with Emotional and Behavioural Difficulties in Primary and Secondary Classrooms.* London: David Fulton.

Ministry of Education (1955) *Report of the Committee on Maladjusted Children.* (Underwood Report). London: HMSO.

Molnar, A. and Lindquist, B. (1989) *Changing Problem Behaviour in Schools.* San Francisco: Jossey Bass.

Moore, T. (1966) 'Difficulties of the ordinary child to adjusting to primary school.' *Journal of Child Psychology and Psychiatry,* 7, 17-38.

National Curriculum Council (1989) *A Curriculum for All: SEN in the National Curriculum.* York: N.C.C.

Norwich, B. (1993) 'The National Curriculum and Special Educational Needs.' In, P. O'Hear. and J. White. *Assessing the National Curriculum.* London: Paul Chapman.

Orr, R. (1995) Prescription for Failure. *Special Children.* September Edn. P24-25.

Peagram, E. (1995) 'The foolish man built his house on sand.' *Therapeutic Care and Education,* 4, 9-16.

Plowden (Chair) (1967) Children and their Primary Schools. *Report of the Central Advisory Council (England).* London: Central Advisory Council.

Reiser, R. (1994) 'Making Sense and Nonsense of the Code of Practice.' *Learning Together,* 2, 4-9.

Rowland, K. and Travell, C. (1995) 'Working with parents, families and carers.' *Emotional and Behavioural Difficulties Distance Education Course, Unit 5.* Birmingham: University of Birmingham Distance Education Unit.

Rutter, M. (1966) Children and sick parents: An environmental and Psychiatric Study. *Maudsley Monograph No. 16.* London: London University Press.

Rutter, M., Tizard, J. and Whitmore, L. (1970) *Health Education and Behaviour.* London: Longman.

Smith, T. (1987) 'Family Centres: prevention, partnerships or community alternatives.' In, McFarlane, J.A. (Ed) *Progress in Child Health Vol 3.* Edinburgh: Churchill Livingstone.

Stakes, J. R. and Hornby, G. (1996) 'Special Needs.' In, R. Andrews (Ed) *Interpreting the New National Curriculum.* Uxbridge: Middlesex University Press.

TES (1998) 'Teenagers time out' 3 vii 1998 p6.

Underwood, (1995) *An Enquiry into the Education of Maladjusted Children.* London: HMSO.

Upton, G. (1996) in G. Upton and V. Varma (Eds) *Stress in SEN Teachers* Aldershot: Arena.

Warnock, M. (1978) *Special Educational Needs: Report of the Committee of Enquiry into the Education of Handicapped Children and Young People.* London: HMSO.

Whitehead, M. 'Bad behaviour now' in *TES* 3 vi 1997.

Wickman, E. K. (1928) *Teacher's reactions to the behaviour problems of children in Children's Behaviour and Teachers' Attitudes.* New York: The Commonwealth Fund.

Wedlock, P. and McCleod, F. (1984) *Raising Standards: Parental Involvement Programmes and the Language of Children.* Coventry: CEDE.

Williamson, H. (1998) 'Places with pupils in their heart.' *Special Children* 12 vi p13.

Woodhead, C. (1997) Annual Report of HMCI. London: OFSTED.

Wolfendale, S. (1992) *Empowering Parents and Teachers: Working for Children.* London: Cassell.

Wolff, S. (1986) *Knowledge and treatment in the practical treatment and understanding of disturbed children, Workshops Perspective 1.* Association of Workers for Maladjusted Children. Maidstone: Association of Maladjusted Children.

Woodcock, C. (1997) *The Guardian/Institute of Education Debate.* Manchester: The Guardian Newspaper.

Wragg, E. C. and Dooley, P. A. (1984) 'Classroom management during teaching practice.' In, E. C. Wragg (Ed). *Classroom Teaching Skills.* London: Croom Helm.

Chapter Six

Thinking through Behaviour Management: principles and practice

by Bill Gribble

> *'A child's current behaviour often reflects an essentially sane response to an untenable set of life circumstances'*
> (Bray, 1997)

For many children, their schooldays are not the happiest days of their lives. Increasingly, children and young people are becoming excluded, or exclude themselves from the process of State Education in the United Kingdom (Parsons, 1996). Schools are increasingly being encouraged to include these same, disaffected children in their classrooms (Welsh Office, 1999). There appears, however, to be too few opportunities for teachers to learn the skills that will enable them to cope with children's behaviour and the continuing changes to, and expectations of, their profession.

At the end of the last decade, the Elton Report (HMSO, 1989) concluded that teachers were not being 'beaten up' by disruptive and violent children, rather they were being 'beaten down' by new initiatives and changes to the curriculum. At the end of this millennium, it seems reasonable to ask the question, how much of this reality has in fact really changed? More importantly too, perhaps, is the related question of how this explanation and others can help teachers and pupils better manage classroom behaviour!

There are no panaceas by which inclusion in the educative process for all children will be achieved. Neither does it appear to be desirable that mainstream schools attempt to educate *all* emotionally and behaviourally disturbed children (Daniels, Visser, Cole & de Reybekill, 1998). There is, however, a real opportunity for schools to become places where a sense of *belonging* can be encouraged in most children and acceptable behaviours can be taught by teachers and colleagues.

Managing behaviour and misbehaviour: a positive approach

Charlton and David (1993) argued that it is possible to manage some of the more extreme or challenging behaviour presented by pupils in the mainstream classroom. Much can be achieved by supportive teachers and schools adopting a positive approach to behaviour management (see Gribble, 1993).

Accepting this premise, and with the aim of developing a system to manage most children's behaviour in mainstream schooling, it is helpful, indeed perhaps necessary, to identify some important points about the management of pupil behaviour in the school context. These include:

- the behaviour of adults who are connected in any way to the school can influence the behaviour of pupils;
- confrontational styles of behaviour management can produce adverse reactions in children;
- observing children's behaviour, in the classroom context, aids adult empathy and planning;
- listening to and consulting with children, parents, colleagues and other agencies involved with the child at school can give everyone an opportunity to understand why a preferred practice is desirable in that context - and perhaps other contexts too;
- adult and child behaviour, that is under control and considers the needs of others, gives everybody more time for their own individual learning needs to be met;
- agreed consequences are more effective and acceptable than punishment.

All parents and teachers will need to come to understand that difficult and disobedient behaviours are part of normal child development. The dilemma for both parent and teacher is which behaviours are just passing phases of naughtiness and which behaviours, if left unchecked, are damaging to children and those around them.

This dilemma has been epitomised by R. D. Laing, one of the best known psychiatrists of our modern times, who observed that:

> *It is our duty to bring up our children to love,*
> *honour and obey us.*
> *If they don't, they must be punished,*
> *otherwise we would not be doing our duty.*

If they grow up to love, honour and obey us
we have been blessed for bringing them up properly

If they grow up not to love, honour and obey us
either we have brought them up properly
or we have not:
if we have
there must be something the matter with them;
if we have not
there must be something the matter with us.

(R. D. Laing 1927-1989)

In this insightful but simple text from Laing's book entitled 'Knots' (1970), Laing presents the parent and teacher with the eternal, ganglionic question, 'Is it me or is it them?' The emotional turmoil created by such questioning and the inherent dilemmas therein, have been the source of much of mankind's philosophical deliberation. Learning from this deliberation appears to form at least one aspect of civilised society's formation of order and good citizenship.

The management of behaviour and the learning process, for those involved in the daily life of the school, appears all too often to be wrapped up in the 'us and them' question of 'blame'. Laing hints in his text that the way forward to resolution will need to be sought in the transaction, not in the people. Perhaps the people involved are just simply people being human, and it is simply their behaviour rather than nature that requires some modification. The way in which we can improve behaviour is very much about how we develop the skills of interaction - for teacher and pupil(s) - there is a need for these skills to be mutually understood, taught or learnt.

It appears necessary, therefore, for those involved in the business of managing these transactions to stand back from the fray of a continuing series of interpersonal relationships and, in some detail, observe the process that is taking place. This is a very difficult position to achieve when you are very close to the process and possibly already 'beaten down' by the daily 'give and take' of working with difficulties or problem behaviour. By adopting this position, however, and observing the process, teachers can begin removing a need for blame and concentrating instead on how the process or transaction can be improved. Organisations such as schools can develop strategies that improve their procedures and transactions, ultimately creating a more positive learning environment.

It is important, too, to remember that each player has a role to play in this drama of social interaction and learning. Furthermore, it is important that each participant knows their place in this scenario, is encouraged to feel safe, secure and confident in themselves and their emotional, social interactional skills, as well as those of the other players. Knowing the script, rehearsing scenes, and preparing for the performance, in terms of behaviour management, are as much appropriate aspects of in-service training aimed at implementing whole-school behaviour policies, as they are for activities more generally aimed at improving teacher's skills, attitudes and competencies.

The ultimate aim for school-based staff, in an ideal world, would be to teach all the adults involved in the school community, their role in these school-based, behavioural transactions. This training would, hopefully, give a level of understanding that equips them with the emotional skills to respond appropriately and with confidence in most behavioural transactions. It would then be possible, in turn, for these adults to become more self-confident, and no longer be in a position when calling a child to account, to think, 'What am I going to say next?'

Schools making the difference

Education, or the teaching of our society's combined knowledge and beliefs, does make a difference for the prospects of a pupil's career (Coleman & Hendry, 1990). However, there are an increasing number of conduits or routes down which the various forms of knowledge can travel. As individuals, we will never control all these conduits. We cannot prevent some aspects of knowledge reaching and influencing our society's children, even though some of this knowledge may be faulty, biased and, at worst, damaging. Figure 1 looks at the variables that appear to influence student achievement. The variables are different for each child as are the conduits reaching them.

Within Student	External to student
Desire to Learn	Quality of Curriculum
Strategies for Learning	Quality of Teaching
Learning Style (academic coping)	Motivation of Teacher
	Pedagogical Knowledge
Alterable	Subject Knowledge
Skills (social coping)	Quality and Type of Evaluation
Prior Content Knowledge	Quality of Learning Environment
Self-Efficacy	Quality of Time Given
Helplessness (perceived or otherwise)	Use Made of Time Allowed
Race (perception of race by others)	
Genetic potential	
Gender	
Unalterable	Family Income and Resources
(Hard to change)	Peer Socio-economic Status
Disposition	Family Housing
Birth Order	Parents' Schooling
Health/Diet	Family Mobility
Physical Differences	Family Siblings and extended
I.Q.	Family Values
E.Q.	Family History
Disability Category	
Personal History	

Figure 1: Variables which influence student achievement (Howell, K., 1998)

Figure 1 illustrates clearly the areas that adults who work with children can influence. It would appear futile and a waste of valuable time, in school, to attempt to influence the areas below the horizontal line - including individual differences which are relatively fixed or are features of family and home environment. As adults who work with children and young people, however, it will be necessary for us to understand the effect that these influences will have upon the individuals we teach. It is important that we are aware and, when necessary, compensate for adverse circumstances or individual difficulty by adjusting those areas above the horizontal line. By altering these areas and adapting them according to the needs of the individuals in our schools, adults involved in the process of teaching and learning will be better equipped when attempting to include more young people in the educational process. This consideration of alterable and unalterable states is similar to the development of personal constructs within an ecosystemic framework.

As teachers and parents, this understanding and development of our skills will assist us in the control and influence over some of the previously described conduits for learning, especially when working with children. The ecosystemic framework appears to offer one opportunity in planning to respond to the behaviours that are the consequence of a wide variety of influences. We may be able to understand some of the influences upon the behaviour of others and through that understanding help them, especially children or young people, come to their own understanding.

It would also seem sensible to acknowledge that some influences affecting student achievement are unalterable and therefore to concentrate on areas where adults in the school context can exert some influence. This clearly seems to be the most appropriate and productive course of action for the practising teacher. As parents, carers and teachers it is also important to understand that, as adults, we have a duty of care (Whitney, 1993). Failure in that duty has grave implications for individuals, education and society. Understanding clearly what our duties are in guiding children along the most appropriate conduits and the influence that we as adults have in that process, are fundamental to both teaching and parenthood.

A professional approach to managing behaviour

Understanding the influences upon behaviour could lead to the conclusion that behaviour is learnt and that observed behaviour is based upon discernible choice. Choice appears fundamental in the process of managing behaviour. If we choose to be in control of our own behaviour and channel it to improve our situation, and if we are successful, we are usually motivated to repeat those behaviours. If, in turn, this motivation is nurtured or rewarded positively, we may even be helped to understand that it is more desirable to work with others, constructively. We can thus achieve more than when working in isolation.

Observing and recording behaviour and subsequently analysing it is an important part of the process. A helpful idea in developing this technique, taken from behavioural psychology, looks at behaviour in terms of ABC; *Antecedents, Behaviours and Consequences.* This key construct can be used to aid an understanding of what it is that drives behaviour in both adults and pupils. Wheldall and Merrett (1984) use this idea in their book to help teachers develop a positive teaching style; a style of teaching that leaves the behaviour and the consequences of that behaviour firmly with the pupil - although it should be immediately acknowledged, this requires great self-control on the part of the teacher.

From day one of my teaching career, I have found it difficult, even undesirable, to control children's behaviour. However, I have learnt that it is self-control that is a most important aspect of classroom management. Bill Rogers in some recent correspondence with me referred to Aristotle's Nicomadiean Ethics, in which he advised mankind to:

> '... not forget that it is human to be painfully affected by anger and to find revenge sweet ... Anyone can become angry - that is easy. But to be angry with the right person, to the right degree, at the right time for the right purpose, and in the right way - this is not easy.'
>
> (Aristotle 385-322 BC)

It would seem that choosing to be in control of one's own behaviour is the preferred state we would wish for both ourselves and our children - even when we are angry and to some extent are 'losing control'. This implies a clear understanding of the options open to us in a given context, in this case the classroom. A teacher or parent, if they are going to give clear messages concerning acceptable and unacceptable behaviours, needs to be rational and controlled in themselves. They are required to understand the social context and teach their children to learn within this context, to get the most out of it, and to develop the necessary behaviours, skills and attitudes they will need to succeed in life.

Teachers, therefore, will need to have a clear vision of what is required in terms of preferred practices in classrooms. Parents will need a similar vision for life at home. This should be an aim for all teachers and parents. A *preferred practice* is the desired behaviour which one wishes to elicit or exhibit in a given context (Rogers, 1995). How often is this vision lost by us all in the daily grind? Through planning and considering the impact of our own behaviours upon others, we can work towards at least two important aspects of these preferred practices. The first preferred practice would be to recover the situation. The second is a consistent method; planning in advance approaches that will consider the clear, consistent, positive messages we wish to give to children.

Applying the professional approach to managing behaviour

Theoretical models are helpful in planning and developing interventions, but which method is best suited to behaviour management in classrooms and school is very much open to debate. Theoretical models do give a direction when managing classroom behaviour. However, having knowledge of the different approaches gives confidence and insight.

The following three theories appear to underpin the key models contained in the literature.

(1) Skinnerian Behaviourism

Rooted in the understanding of 'STIMULUS-RESPONSE', this approach has been used by experimenters to elicit the desired behaviour in human beings and animals by ignoring unwanted behaviour and rewarding desired behaviour.

(2) Freudian Psychoanalysis

This is a child-centred approach historically used by Child Guidance. Results are derived from in-depth analysis of individual therapy sessions. This approach requires co-operation and a great deal of time.

(3) Rogerian Counselling

A 'self-concept' theory that allows the subject to come to an understanding of self through empathy and realisation of potential.

Which psychological approach is best suited to the classroom has been the subject of enquiry and empirical research. Kolvin (1981) in the Newcastle Study, evaluated the three theories and came to the conclusion that in some cases the very fact of any type of referral for treatment had a positive effect and that it was working directly with children which appeared to be more important than a single model. The results suggested that an eclectic approach was the best basis for the development of classroom-based interventions.

Topping (1983), in a study of cost-effectiveness, found that the more expensive interventions were not necessarily the more effective. Topping further reported that it appeared there was a 66% spontaneous remission rate in populations of severely disruptive and delinquent adolescents. This remission occurred no matter what type of intervention was undertaken.

Topping (1983) compared the success rates of various support programmes to the phenomenon of spontaneous remission. He suggested that the identification of the source of problematic behaviour was the first step towards securing a resolution of the problem. Another way this might be expressed is that we need to observe the behaviour in context and the emotions exhibited in order to understand the behaviour produced prior to attempting an intervention.

Rayner (1998), in his analysis of the education of pupils with emotional and behaviour difficulties, suggests that it is an eclectic pedagogy that is the key in managing classroom behaviour. An example of one practical, eclectic approach is that postulated by Cooper and Upton (1990). They utilised the theory associated with an ecosystemic model, an approach previously identified as a strategic approach to planning intervention. Within the ecosystemic framework, problem behaviour is not seen as originating from within pupils but from within the interaction between pupils and the adults in the school context. The approach concentrates upon the process, not the 'us and them'.

When employing an ecosystemic approach in managing classroom and whole school behaviour, the teacher (and any other adult in the school) uses personal constructs or perceptions set against the constructs of others in the social system. This involves the teacher in a degree of self-analysis and creates opportunities to break cycles of behaviour that could otherwise become entrenched.

Another example of an eclectic approach, one of many, is that postulated by Bill Rogers (Rogers, 1994). His general model for school discipline and classroom management is described as a positive approach to managing behaviour. Roger's eclectic and pragmatic ideas, influenced by the work of Dreikurs (Dreikurs, Grunwald & Pepper, 1982) and Kounin (1979) reflected similar thinking found in Topping's early work (Topping, 1983). Topping suggested that by merely concentrating on positive language, the adults who work with children in schools can make a positive difference to the exhibited behaviour. Topping concluded that children in an environment of positive language were, subsequently, more likely to realise a mutual understanding of what is acceptable classroom behaviour.

EBD and a positive response

In what many might perceive as an increasingly troubled society, children and young people with emotional and behavioural difficulties form the largest and fastest growing Special Needs group (Webb, 1992; Parsons, 1996). *The Education Act 1993* has to some extent institutionalised the EBD child by creating Pupil Referral Units. Underlying factors such as why there are a growing number of EBD pupils in our society do not appear to be successfully addressed. Nevertheless, the *Education Act 1996* and the 1997 Supplement went further than any other legislation in imposing a duty on schools and Local Education Authorities to include all pupils in the educative process, and as far as possible in mainstream school settings. The process of planning, strategy formation and target setting were at the heart of this legislation.

The Welsh Office (1999) White Paper on Special Education recently reiterated this position. The Social Inclusion Government Think Tank has currently, at its policy core, education and training as the vehicle for bringing back into our society disaffected young people. 'New Start' and 'Youth Access' are products of this drive. The newly formed Youth Offender Teams, and cross-County Council Agencies and Departments see 'citizenship' and 'acceptable conduct in the community' as an aim of education. Currently, interest and demands, generated largely by what appears is a quest for an appropriate, cost-effective education system by central Government, offers educationists an opportunity to reflect on our present management practices in school and capitalise on the best practice. It is also the case that recent Government guidance is increasingly taking a similar line, reflecting the attempt to identify and disseminate good practice (see, for example, Daniels et al, 1998; QCA /DfEE, 1999).

Planning for and developing an appropriate curriculum, based upon the emotional as well as academic needs of pupils, appears to be the key to the complex issue of classroom behaviour management (see Greenhalgh, 1994). Planning for behaviour by Local Education Authorities (LEAs), through the framework of an LEA Behaviour Support Plan has already been reported in the national press, in statistical terms, to have reduced the need to permanently exclude children in some LEAs from mainstream schooling. If this trend continues, reinforced by the legislative requirement for all schools to develop both comprehensive Behaviour Support Plans and Home-School Agreements, as part of a wider consultation with parents, children, governors, teachers, adults in school and the LEA, then children and young people should get an education which they value better as well as one which is of best value!

As a foundation for this effective education, a positive management approach can be better enabled by providing steps of success in a framework for pupils experiencing behavioural difficulties and disaffection. Schools can actively and directly help pupils experiencing difficulty or failure regain self-respect and, above all, dignity. Within a supportive education system, pupils will develop self-esteem and hopefully enter society as 'full citizens' because they have been taught and see the need to be such a citizen.

One example of a specific class-based approach reflecting this kind of positive approach which is process-centred is 'circle time'. Jenny Mosley (1999) in developing a 'Circle Time' approach, i.e. a method for securing the empowerment of children and young people as an aid in helping them understand their behaviour and the behaviour of others, has described the development of self-esteem and self-discipline as an essential element in this process. The approach is aimed at developing a system of classroom and school behaviour management that nurtures direct 'involvement' and 'ownership' of the process by pupils, while overlapping with other areas of learning activity within the classroom.

An indication of the importance of an understanding of self-esteem and self-discipline as an aspect of the protocols required in developing such a system of positive behaviour management is presented by Bill Rogers in his book 'Behaviour Management' (Rogers, 1995). A protocol, in this sense, is a term used to describe one or more principles that we agree to observe as teachers in school, working with both colleagues and pupils. Following such principles makes us professional in our interaction with our pupils. Instead of relying on our personality or power, we can genuinely and humanely maintain good relationships in the classroom and guide pupils towards self-controlled behaviour. Rogers (1998) later referred to these protocols as *preferred practices*.

In the context of a positive approach to classroom management, teachers and colleagues in school should, according to Rogers (1995), develop protocols that:

- Establish mutually agreed *rights, responsibilities,* and *rules.*
- Always attempt to minimise *hostility* and *embarrassment.*
- Maximise the possibility of *choice.*
- Develop and maintain *respect* through self-discipline and control.
- *Follow up* and *follow through.*
- Avoid disappointment, make sure you can *deliver promises.*
- Maintain a sense of *balance* (humour?).
- Encourage *support* from and for your friends and colleagues to enhance opportunities for self-worth and self-esteem.
- Personally, seek to *lower stress* levels.

Figure 2: Protocols involved in classroom management

Protocols help maintain the dignity of the teacher/adult and pupil/ child. A professional dignity can arise from a balanced observation of these protocols in the relationship or transaction between the teacher/adult and the pupil/child (see Farrell, 1995; Mosley, 1999). This balance may be achieved by developing 'mutual respect' between the participants involved in any teaching and learning event within the school context.

At a whole school level, the creation of a behaviour management policy is now a legal requirement. The DfE Circulars on Pupils with Problems, commonly referred to as the 'six-pack' (DfE, 1994), strongly recommended that successful whole-school policies for behaviour management should contain the following features:

- be simple and straightforward, and be based on a clear and defensible set of principles or values;
- mutual respect is a useful starting point (this phrase was used in the guidance document, DfE, 1993, *Pupils with Problems,* but did not appear in the final guidance Circular 8/94);
- provide for the punishment of bad behaviour and encourage good behaviour;
- be specific to the school and/or classroom/situation (Annex DfE Circular: 8/94, 1994);
- rules should be kept to the minimum necessary to ensure good behaviour;
- the reasons for each rule should be clear;
- wherever possible rules should be expressed in positive, constructive terms, although it should be absolutely clear what pupils are not allowed to do.

In order to maintain the dignity of both teacher and pupil, it is important to maintain a balanced view of the *politics*, *principles* and *practicalities* of the educational settings in which sets of behaviour are exhibited (Gribble, 1993). These aspects of human interaction are necessary considerations, especially in the context of the school. They are equally important considerations in the development and implementation of a behaviour management policy. It is almost as simple as and just like saying 'get real' if you want it to actually 'work'.

Finally, it is important to remember that the organisation and effect of management structures in school will greatly effect the ethos and success of behaviour management. All the theoretical knowledge and rhetoric available, and focused upon a single issue or problem, will not overcome a particular set of attitudes, particularly attitudes perpetuated by senior management. The politics of the social context need to be understood in this situation. Changing the attitudes of fellow professionals may be very difficult but not insurmountable if the parameters are known and the political system that distributes the power is understood. Postman and Weingartner (1976) suggested that school teachers have a responsibility to provide the young with a 'What is it good for?' perspective on their own society.

Authority and regard: are there dangers in delivering discipline?

Is discipline a dirty word? Discipline, like most words in our language, has many connotations. In Latin, 'disciplina' means teaching. In its proper sense, then, and understood to refer to self-control, order, and the opportunity to teach, rather than correction or punishment, this concept lies at the heart of the perspective on behaviour management presented in this chapter. Furthermore, establishing appropriate relationships, agreeing rights and demarcating responsibilities are perceived as essential features of effective discipline. While boundaries and firmness are aspects of developing a framework for discipline, so too is an emphasis upon flexibility, genuineness and regard for pupils by the teacher.

Ensuring authority as an exercise may be likened to commanding respect, it is a commodity which is earned rather than obtained by demand. A good manager will exercise discipline and control in such a way that those who are managed are part of the process which sees respect grow. A dogged entrenchment during classroom transactions, either by the teacher or the pupil, inevitably resulting in confrontation does cause tension in the learning situation (Parsons & Howlett, 1996). This directly affects the relationship between both pupils and teacher as well as impacting upon learning performance. Compromise, if possible by negotiation, is a more preferred course of action (Charlton & David, 1993). This compromise should *not* be a win or lose transaction but should be based upon prior, agreed and understood principles.

This realisation by the adults involved in the teaching-learning relationship is what Rogers (1995) called *preferred practice*. Preferred practices, principles or protocols are established and agreed by those affected by them. It is essential that principles are developed in consultation with the protagonists who will use them, especially in the context of the school. To miss out on this consultation upon the principles involved in a learning process will result in an imposed system. It has been shown that imposed systems result in a lack of ownership by those affected by them. This results in the principles being ignored. Tension and conflict of this kind is often more widely referred to as **stress**. The greatest reported cause of stress in classroom teachers is the disruption caused by some pupils (Rogers, 1992).

Coping with personal stress and coming to a state where self-control is achieved by both teacher and pupil underpins what has earlier been termed a **positive approach** to classroom behaviour management. This approach looks for and rewards 'on task' behaviour and attempts a least-to-most intrusive approach. The teacher or adult involved in the teaching-learning relationship is aware and sensitive to the need to match the seriousness of disruptive behaviour by the child to their preplanned and agreed response. This eclectic approach does not seek to *own* a student's behaviour but does seek to assist the student in owning their own behaviour, whilst at the same time being in full control of that same behaviour.

In a very real and pragmatic way, this approach is a good example of a practical application of a theoretical model. Maintaining dignity in the classroom requires a balance of what is politic, what is agreed in principle and what can be done in immediate, specifically pragmatic terms. This understanding gives a new confidence and a feeling of self-worth which should make the classroom a more effective and enjoyable place to be for both teacher and student.

Although not yet legislative, the Draft Guidance on Social Inclusion: Pupil Support (DfEE, 1999) will undoubtedly underpin Government, and in turn OHMCI's as well as OFSTED's expectation of classroom behaviour planning. Whole school behaviour management policies, home-school agreements, the inclusion of EBD pupils in mainstream schooling and the development of inter-agency partnerships will be informed by further research and guidance sponsored by the DfEE. One such example is the research looking at the provision for EBD in mainstream schools, recently completed by Daniels et al (1998). The report stated that 'staff must "live" agreed policy and desired values', giving clear direction and advice to all personnel working in school and classrooms. It concluded that it is the consistent application of agreed policy, by adherence to and an understanding of the politics, principles and practicalities, which is crucial in an effective provision for pupils with EBD.

It is interesting to consider alternatively the perspectives of pupils and teachers when asked about the question of behaviour management and problems in the classroom. Pupils, in their comments to the research team in the previously mentioned research (Daniels et al, 1998), when describing what made good staff, suggested that the following aspects of teacher behaviour were of greatest importance:

- teachers who understand you and take an interest in you;
- after you have finished your work they ask how you are;
- they socialise with us;
- you get to like them.

In research carried out in the special school context (Cole, Visser & Upton, 1998), teachers expressed an opinion that staff who are effective at managing classroom behaviour show that they are:

- confident, yet have humility;
- genuine;
- able to and do develop warm relationships with pupils;
- listeners;
- those who exhibit care and understanding;
- the ones who receive and use appropriate physical contact to good effect.

If it is appropriate to draw any conclusion with regard to managing children's behaviour in the classroom, it can be argued that by understanding the politics, principles and practicalities that pertain in their schools and their classrooms, teachers and other adults in schools can develop transactions with pupils that constantly communicate desired behaviours clearly and with consistency, conviction and care. By adopting a decisive teaching style that, firstly, establishes authority and secondly, conveys regard, adults in the school context can learn to respect students, even if they do not like them!

Conclusion

Pragmatically, for adults in school to manage personal stress and to develop self-control in themselves and students, there needs to exist an open culture which recognises, analyses, records and evaluates behaviour in a management framework. A convenient and successful template for such a culture is identified in this chapter as the model of assessment and intervention built around the idea of A-ANTECEDENT; B-BEHAVIOUR; C-CONSEQUENCES. This cycle of planning is necessary in many aspects of school development and should generally underpin school development planning.

Planning by adults in school through the development of strategies to deal with unwanted behaviour, that is, using a *rights*, *responsibility*, *rules*, *recovery* focus (prior to the need for its use), should underpin this planning. However, to undertake this planning in isolation and without consulting the client groups of children, teachers, governors, parents/carers and local authority could result in an imposition. Such a policy in its implementation will not last, because it is not understood or owned. Further, such planning should also include a consideration of the emotional development and well-being that exists in both adult and child. It will be necessary to teach and learn the emotional as well as the practical skills and enhance them through this planning process, if there is to be real hope of success, and the realisation of effective education through the positive management of pupil behaviour.

References

Bernard M. E., Joyce M. R. and Rosewarne P.M. (1983), 'Helping teachers cope with stress: a rational-emotive approach.' In A. Ellis and M. E. Bernard (eds). *Rational - emotive approaches to the problems of childhood.* pp 415-467 New York: Pelum Press.

Bernard, M. E. (1987) *Staying Rational in an Irrational World. Albert Ellis and rational-emotive therapy.* McCulloch-Macmillan, Melbourne: Australia.

Berne, E. (1976) *Games People Play: The Psychology of Human Relationships.* Harmondsworth: Penguin Psychology and Psychiatry.

Bible Societies (1994 ed.) New Life Good News Bible, Paul's Second Letter to the Corinthians, Chap. 2 Verse 7. London: Harper Collins.

Bower, E. M. (1969) *Early identification of emotionally handicapped children in school.* Springville, Ill.: Charles C. Thomas.

Bray, M. (1997) *Sexual Abuse: The Child's Voice* - 'Poppies on the Rubbish Heap' London: Jessica Kingsley.

Charlton, T. and David, K. (Eds) (1993) *Managing Misbehaviour in Schools* (2nd. Ed.) London: Routledge.

Chisholm, B., Kearney, D., Knight, H., Little, H., Morris, S. and Tweddle, D. (1986) *Preventive Approaches to Disruption (PAD).* Basingstoke: Macmillan.

Colby D. and Harper T. (1985) *Preventing Classroom Disruption.* London: Croom Helm.

Cole, T., Visser, J. and Upton, G. (1998) *Effective Schooling for Pupils with Emotional and Behavioural Difficulties.* London: David Fulton.

Coleman, J. C. and Hendry, L. (1990) *The Nature of Adolescence (2nd Ed).* London: Routledge.

Cooper, P. and Upton, G. (1990) 'An ecosystemic approach to emotional and behavioural difficulties in schools.' *Educational Psychology,* 10 (4): pp301-21.

Daniels, H., Visser, J., Cole, T. and de Reybekill, N. (1998) *Emotional and Behavioural Difficulties in Mainstream Schools, DfEE Research Report No 90.* London: HMSO.

Department for Education (1994) Pupils with Problems, Circular 8/94, '*Pupil Behaviour and Discipline*'; Section: Whole-school Behaviour Policies and Approaches; Para 20, p11.

Department for Education (1993) Pupils with Problems: Draft Guidance Circulars. London: DfE.

Department for Education and Employment (DfEE), (1999) Draft Guidance, Social Inclusion: Pupil Support. London: HMSO.

Department of Education and Science (1978) *Special Educational Needs (The Warnock Report).* London: HMSO.

Department of Education and Science (1981) *Education Act (1981) Special Education.* London HMSO.

Department of Education and Science (1986) *Education (No. 2) Act 1986.* London: HMSO.

Department of Education and Science (1989) Circular 22/89/ Welsh Office Circular 54/89, *Assessments and Statement of Special Educational Needs: Procedures within the Education, Health and Social Services* (Annex to HN989 20/HN(FP)19/LASSL(89)7WOC54/89). London: HMSO.

Dreikurs, R., Grunwald, B. and Pepper, F. (1982) *Maintaining Sanity in the Classroom.* New York: Harper and Row.

Education Reform Act 1998. London: HMSO.

Elton Report. (1989) *Discipline in Schools.* Report by the Committee of Enquiry chaired by Lord Elton. London: HMSO

Farrell, P. (1995) 'Guidelines for Helping Children with Emotional and Behavioural Difficulties.' In, P. Farrell (Editor) *Children with Emotional and Behavioural Difficulties.* London: Falmer Press.

Galloway D. and Goodwin C. (1987) *The Education of Disturbing Children.* Harlow: Longman.

Glasser, W. (1986) *Control Theory in the Classroom.* New York: Harper & Row.

Greenhalgh, P. (1994) *Emotional Growth and Learning.* London: Routledge.

Gribble, G. W. (1989) *Behavioural Support in a High School.* Unpublished M.Ed Thesis, School of Education, University College of North Wales. Bangor: University College of North Wales.

Gribble, G. W. (1993) 'Keeping our heads above water.' *Special Children,* October, pp14 -15.

Gribble, G. W. (1993) *Behaviour Management for Teachers: A Positive Approach to Discipline in Schools.* Bangor: School of Education, University of Wales.

Hargreaves, D. H. (1972) *Interpersonal Relationships in Education.* Routledge: Kogan Paul.

HMSO (1989) Discipline in Schools, report by the Committee of Enquiry chaired by Elton. London: HMSO.

Howell, K. (1998) 'Variables which influence student achievement.' In, B. Rogers. *Behaviour Recovery, (2nd Edition).* Harlow: Longman.

Kolvin, I. (1981) *Help Starts Here.* London: Tavistock

Kounin, J. S. (1979) *Discipline and Group Management in Classrooms.* New York: Rinehart and Winston.

Laing, R. D. (1970) *Knots.* Harmondsworth: Penguin - Psychology and Psychiatry.

Masson J. (1990) *The Children Act 1989: text and commentary.* London: Sweet and Maxwell.

McNamara, S. and Moreton, G. (1996) *Changing Behaviour: Teaching Children with Emotional and Behavioural Difficulties in Primary and Secondary Classrooms.* London: David Fulton.

Mosley, J. (1999) *More Quality Circle Time.* Cambs: LDA.

Parsons, C. (1996) *Final Report on Follow-up Survey of Permanent Exclusion from Schools in England - 1995/96.* Canterbury: Christ Church College.

Parsons, C. and Howlett, K. (1996) 'Permanent Exclusion from School: A Case Where Society is Failing its Children.' *Support for Learning,* 11, 3, 109-112.

Pearce, J. (1989) *Bad Behaviour: How to deal with naughtiness and disobedience and still show you love and care for your child.* London: Thorsons Publishing Group.

Postman, N. and Weingartner, C. (1976) *Teaching as a Subversive Activity.* Harmondsworth: Penguin Education Specials.

QCA/DfEE (1999) *Supporting the Target Setting Process: guidance for effective target setting for pupils with special educational needs.* London: DfEE.

Rayner, S. (1998) 'Educating Pupils with Emotional and Behaviour Difficulties: Pedagogy is the Key!' *Emotional and Behavioural Difficulties,* 3, 2, 39-47.

Reid, K. (1986) *Disaffection from School.* London: Methuen.

Robertson, J. (1990) *Effective Classroom Control.* London: Hodder and Stoughton (Educational).

Rogers, B. (1989) *Decisive Discipline: Every Move You Make, Every Step You Take (A video learning package).* Geelong, Victoria, Australia: The Institute of Educational Administration.

Rogers, B. (1990) *You Know the Fair Rule.* Victoria, Australia: Australian Council for Educational Research.

Rogers, B. (1992) *Managing Teacher Stress.* London: Pitman Publishing.

Rogers, B. (1994) *The Language of Discipline.* Plymouth: Northcote House.

Rogers, B. (1995) *Behaviour Management: A whole-school approach.* Melbourne, Australia: Ashton Scholastic.

Rogers, B.(1998) *Behaviour Recovery.* Harlow: Longman.

Rutter, M., Maughan, B., Mortimore, P. and Ouston, J. (1979) *Fifteen Thousand Hours.* London: Open Books.

Topping, K. (1983) *Educational Systems for Disruptive Adolescents.* London: Croom Helm.

Trowell, J. and Bower, M. (1995) *The Emotional Needs of Children and Their Families: Using Psychoanalytic Ideas in the Community* (Chapter 4. pgs 38-53). London: Routledge.

Webb, S. (1992) 'Helping Troublesome Children.' In, *Croner's Head Teacher's Bulletin,* November, pp3-4.

Welsh Office (1999) *Shaping the Future for Special Education - An Action Programme for Wales: The BEST Programme, Building Excellent Schools Together.* Cardiff: The Welsh Office.

Wheldall K. and Merrett F. (1984) *Positive Teaching, The Behavioural Approach.* London: Unwin Education Books.

Whitney, B. (1993) *The Children Act and Schools.* London: Kogan Page.

Wilson, M. and Evans, M. (1980) *Education of Disturbed Pupils, Schools Council Working Paper 65.* London: Methuen.

Chapter Seven

Institutional Interventions

by John Visser

Introduction

A chapter covering all institutional interventions for pupils with EBD is an impossible task. This chapter outlines some of the main issues and hopefully provides the reader with sufficient references to pursue particular aspects.

Pupils with emotional and behavioural difficulties often challenge institutional systems, processes and procedures. They provide the greatest challenge to those who wish to adopt inclusive policies and practices. They are often the cause of the stress that adults within the institutions experience. These pupils are in every form of educational institution sometimes by deliberate placement, as in the case of specialist provision, but more often they are to be found in mainstream schools. The intervention strategies used by these institutions are the subject of this chapter.

A word of caution on these interventions needs to be made at the outset. Topping (1983) refers to 'growth unhampered by evaluation' when he discusses the range of provision he found for pupils with EBD. The fact is that all too often interventions are not based upon evidence of successful outcomes over time. Intervention techniques and strategies commonly used by teachers in the classroom, administrators in deciding placement, and politicians in creating policies are problem-focused rather than solution-focused. They tend to be reactions to perceived challenges rather than worked out interventions based upon secure evidence of what can achieve good outcomes from previous instances. Problem-focused interventions have been found not to have positive results; indeed they often reinforce disruptive behaviour and exacerbate the emotional condition of the child. For example, teachers who make frequent disciplinary interventions both disrupt the class's attention and created a negative atmosphere (Rutter, Maughan, Mortimore & Ouston, 1979). Lines, detentions and punishment exercises have no effect on enabling pupils to behave more appropriately (Topping, 1983). Counselling, too, has been criticised as relatively ineffective. There is little substantive evidence that exclusion is an effective sanction: removing a disruptive child does nothing to help the child and has not been shown to improve the behaviour of those left behind (DES, 1989a; Topping, 1990).

Forms of intervention - forms of institution

The range of institutions where pupils with EBD are to be found is quite large. Within education there are special schools which provide residential provision and some which function as day schools. The residential school will vary between those which offer 52 week placement and those which operate weekly boarding. Then there is the range of provision covered by the phrase 'Education Otherwise'. These include pupil referral units (PRUs) as well as home tuition and hospital schools. This is merely an illustrative list to which of course you should add mainstream schools. Within other agencies there are children's homes, and various forms of juvenile detention centres. Whilst this chapter concentrates upon the interventions within education it also acknowledges that many of the interventions described are common across the range of provision.

Children in EBD special schools amount to only approximately 0.15% of the school-age population (Visser & Cole, 1996) but the benefits of this form of intervention in meeting the needs of pupils with EBD have been challenged (e.g. Topping, 1983; Galloway & Goodwin, 1987). Laslett (1977), Wilson and Evans (1980), Cooper (1993), Grimshaw with Berridge (1994) and Jenkinson (1997) note the practical value of special schools as an option where appropriate. The Warnock Committee (DES, 1978) and DfEE (1997) see the need for their retention as part of a continuum of provision available for children with EBD. Cole, Visser and Upton (1998) show the current range of interventions which are to be found in special school for pupils with EBD. Their report of effective schooling was the first overview of interventions for 20 years and illustrates the point Topping (1983) makes regarding the lack of an evidence-based approach to interventions for pupils with EBD.

There is even less evidence of the benefits of special day units (Tattum,1989). DES (1989b) did note the positive relationships existing in many units and recent OFSTED reports of PRUs have also been more positive. However, this form of intervention is more difficult to justify. Topping (1983) suggests that there is little evidence of pupils improving their learning and academic achievements while attending such units or of successful reintegration after they leave. As Ogilvy (1994) indicates, this form of intervention allows schools to 'off load' children rather than seeing themselves as a part of the problem which the children are manifesting.

Interventions within social services and juvenile justice have similar histories to education. That is, they have been subject to the prevailing whim of administrators, policy makers and, occasionally, well-meaning philanthropists. Laslett, Cooper, Maras, Rimmer & Law (1998) describe this historical development of institutional interventions and rightly refer to 'changing perceptions' rather than accumulation of evidence as to what 'worked' as the overriding reason forms of intervention changed.

Traditional forms of intervention have been largely problem-focused. Having identified a problem the focus has been upon resolving that problem usually by some form of 'punishment'. The range of alternative interventions, largely developed by special schools (Cole et al, 1998), has begun to work its way into more mainstream practices in meeting the needs of pupils with EBD. Garner and Gains (1996) list three major principal theoretical models for intervention in EBD:

- behavioural approaches;
- psychodynamic approaches;
- ecosystemic approaches.

These theoretical approaches are discussed in detail in Apter (1982); Reinert and Huang (1987); Cooper, Smith & Upton (1994); and Ayers, Clarke & Murray (1995) and have been covered elsewhere within this book.

The most widespread intervention strategies used by institutions are those based upon behavioural approaches. Wheldall and Merrett (1992) give an excellent and detailed explanation of this approach. It also underpins the intervention known as assertive discipline which has received some support in recent Government documents (DfEE, 1998). 'Behaviour modification' was criticised by Warnock (DES, 1978) and is considered by some to be incapable of securing long-term improvement in difficult behaviour.

Psychodynamic approaches to problem behaviour, Greenhalgh (1994) argues, show that even the earliest experiences of children will have an influence upon their subsequent behaviour. As psychodynamic approaches are invariably medium to long-term initiatives they are more difficult strategies for mainstream teachers to implement. Greenhalgh (1994) makes a very strong case in his descriptions of the various strategies which have a psychodynamic basis for their inclusion within the broad and balanced curriculum, to which every pupil is entitled.

Ecosystemic approaches to EBD argue that all children belong to a set of social subsystems and that their behaviour is a product of interactions between and within these systems. This approach has its roots in the work of Bronfenbrenner (1979) and Molnar and Lindquist (1989), who observe that teachers and institutions help to maintain a problem by frozen perceptions of the child's past behaviour. Daniels, Visser, Cole with de Reybekill (1999) and Cooper et al (1994) indicate how this intervention strategy can be used with schools. Daniels et al (1999) in particular propose a model which indicates how the various parts of an institution's work can contribute to the meeting of pupils EBD needs in an ecosystemic manner. These writers indicate that where staff can re-frame their interpretations of the pupil's behaviour, they remove blame from the equation, avoid conflict and contribute to finding a solution at the level of understanding the nature of the mismatched subsystems.

It should be noted, however, that any search for one single solution for dealing with the wide range of behaviours associated with EBD is likely to be futile. Any intervention should be eclectic in nature and include the following:

- identification;
- assessment;
- strategy formulation;
- intervention;
- evaluation.

Failure to include any of these jeopardises the potential of the intervention (Ayers et al, 1995).

Whole school policies
Many institutions have behaviour policies as the basis upon which their interventions are made. If policy articulates an institution's intent, then practice shows the extent to which a 'critical mass' of support has been reached among staff and pupils which will allow the policy to work (Gustavsen, 1996). All too frequently, as Nanton (1995) observes, policy is formulaic and tokenistic. Without consultation and user involvement in

policy development, ownership and observance will be small (Fullan, 1993; McGilchrist, Mortimore, Savage & Beresford,1995).

The Elton Report (DES, 1989a), OFSTED guidance (1993) Circular 10/99 (Social inclusion: Pupil Support, DfEE, 1999) and writers such as Clarke and Murray (1996) indicate the need for institutions to have positive whole school behaviour policies. Good practice in these institutions suggests that the senior managers do not rely solely upon verbal communication and modelling of the behaviour policy. They have constructed a clear, accessible document which provides the rationale for the behaviour policy as well as the practical details of how it is to be implemented. In doing this senior staff have involved all members of the institution in contributing to and thus taking ownership of the policy. Such policies according to Daniels et al (1999) cover the following areas:

- the general aims of the school;
- a description of the rights and responsibilities of staff, pupils and parents;
- Code of Conduct/school rules;
- how the institution will encourage good behaviour;
- routines and staff responsibilities;
- sanction and rewards systems;
- pastoral support;
- links to other school policies;
- working with parents.
(Daniels et al, 1999, p25)

The importance of pupils being involved with the creation and maintenance of behaviour policies, and thus the forms of intervention which an institution undertakes, is stressed by a number of writers. It is actively encouraged within the *Code of Practice* (DES, 1994). Meighan and Toogood (1992) propose smaller but highly participatory school communities than are currently commonplace. In so doing, they inform some of the more recent work in this field. Cooper (1996) notes that it is essential to develop participatory democracy in schools for the following reasons:

- pupils are preparing for responsible adult life in a democracy;
- pupils are key players in the success of the school;
- pupils are the majority in school and their voice should be heard (p193).

The evidence suggests that such participation and involvement does take place. Where pupils have been consulted about the formulation of policy, there have been very positive benefits for children with EBD and the incidence of disruptive behaviour has diminished (Coulby & Coulby, 1989; Cole et al, 1998; Daniels et al, 1999).

Long (1999) goes into detail as to how such policies can be created. He provides a useful list of four principles for understanding behaviour which underpin good practice when intervening to meet the needs of pupils with EBD:

- the pupil is not the problem, his/her behaviour is;
- behaviour is functional - it serves a purpose;
- pupils are capable of changing their behaviour;
- behaviour is often an outward display of an inward emotional state.

These principles can be seen to provide guidance when considering interventions in the classroom as well as within the institution.

Intervention strategies - curriculum, teaching and systems

There are a wide range of factors within institutions which can be altered to meet the needs of pupils with EBD. They can be grouped around three areas:

- how the curriculum could be adapted or changed;
- how the teaching could be adapted or improved;
- internal structures and procedures.

Curriculum

Lund (1990) notes that 'most workers now see the child's difficulties as a function of inappropriate curriculum'. This is to overstate the agreement in this area (see Orr, 1995, for an opposing view) but the significance of the curriculum - especially since the *1988 Education Reform Act* introduced a National Curriculum - is now seen of substantial importance (Cole et al, 1998).

Chamberlin and Chamberlin (1993) make the case for reappraising traditional approaches to curricula. They indicate that mainstream schools over-concentrate upon the academic subjects to the detriment of social, moral and emotional areas. Thus, pupils who come to school with needs in these areas tend to experience considerable failure in cognitive areas.

Topping (1983) is one of many authorities to signal problems with curricular provision, noting that failure to cater for learning difficulties may be a significant cause of disruptive behaviour. There have been many calls for alternative curricula for Key Stage 4 pupils in particular (Reid, 1987; Peagram, 1995). These writers perceive a National Curriculum to be inappropriate in meeting the needs of pupils with EBD. The argument for an alternative curriculum seldom addresses the issue of how this could also be inclusive. Nor do those who put forward these arguments address the need for educators to examine their teaching strategies to meet the learning needs and styles of their pupils.

Laslett (1995) echoing Greenhalgh (1994) argues that pupils with EBD need more than just the National Curriculum:

> 'They need to learn about themselves, about other people, about their feelings and behaviour. This learning goes on in countless interchanges...and it goes on more effectively in an environment which recognises its importance.' (p.8)

But note that the argument is not to exempt the pupils with EBD from access to a National Curriculum which is broad and balanced.

The importance of such social and emotional learning as an intervention strategy, necessitates the promotion of whole school policies which recognise that all children are entitled to a curriculum which enhances emotional and social learning.

Schools which differentiate their curriculum to take account of different levels of academic ability, and incorporate their recognition of the importance of psychological, moral and emotional development prominently in curricular provision, will be developing significant positive aids for the development of all children, including those with EBD.

Teaching

Pupils with EBD are a diverse group but have some common traits when it comes to their experience of learning. They often lack interpersonal skills, and are easily frustrated. Attention spans may be short with low anger thresholds, new work is often viewed as frightening and they have an exaggerated dislike of being exposed to tasks which show up their weaknesses. All these factors and more will contribute to the pupils' sense of low academic esteem. They also present teachers with a challenge for their teaching.

Daniels et al (1998) found that the following factors were associated with lessons where pupils with EBD were motivated and engaged in the tasks:

- good classroom control;
- good subject knowledge;
- well planned and differentiated;
- provided achievable challenges;
- provided *some* pupil choice;
- utilised pupil interest and were relevant;
- contained small achievable tasks;
- were not overburdened with writing tasks;
- contained a practical element.

These factors also occur in other writers' lists (see, for example, Cole et al, 1998, for a list associated with good teaching in special schools) and notably the Framework for Inspection (OFSTED, 1995).

Teachers are also very aware of the need to group children and seat them in ways to minimise disruption and maximise co-operation. They use positive peer pressure to encourage good behaviour, as well as seating pupils from time to time by themselves.

Effective institutional intervention with pupils with EBD depends heavily on the experience, personalities and value systems of those employed to work with them. The Underwood Report (Ministry of Education, 1955) stressed that 'the right qualities of character and personality are essential; no training, however thorough, can be a substitute for them'. Wilson and Evans (1980) concurred as did Cole et al (1998).

Cooper et al (1994) stress the importance of teacher style and approach. To this Riding and Rayner (1998) add the need for teachers of young people with EBD to appreciate the learning styles of their pupils. The nature of teacher style and the need for staff to understand pupil learning style was further explored in EBD special schools by Cole et al (1998). They concluded that Government and HMI advice (e.g. Circulars 8 and 9/94, DfEE, 1994; Bull, 1995) was essentially correct. What was required was not so much a drastic alteration of curriculum content as the application of good teaching skills. Good teaching as an intervention followed the basic teaching skills identified in many texts (e.g. Kounin, 1970; Montgomery, 1989; Stone, 1990; Kyriacou, 1991; Smith and Laslett, 1993). Good teachers were also aware of the need to provide differentiated teaching that matched individual needs (Visser, 1993).

Teachers practising in the above manner tended to form positive relationships with pupils with EBD which in turn leads to productive teaching and learning experiences. An essential feature of this practice is that teachers are concerned with the affective needs of the individual child, as well as the attainment of instrumental goals by groups of children (Galloway, 1990; Cooper, 1993; Greenhalgh, 1994; Stoll and Fink, 1994).

Internal structures and procedures

Does size of institution matter? This is often at the back of questions regarding the challenges which institutions face when they identify pupils with EBD. Garbarino (1980) reported research that suggested that large schools depersonalised staff, making them less innovative, less responsive to children's needs, and excessively impersonal. Large schools were also found to concentrate excessively on achieving instrumental goals and failed to involve the 'marginal students' in extra-curricular activities which can give a sense of self-worth and belonging. Yarworth and Gauthier (1978) linked the level of children's self-concept with the extent they participated in school activities. Again, the 'academically marginal' pupils tended to participate less. So size can impact on pupils. What appears from the research to be important is how institutions manage their size to maintain a sense of individual personal worth. Alongside this is the need to clearly identify those pupils for whom coping with the size of the school is a problem. It is as well to remember that this issue cuts both ways. Too big can be an issue, but so can too small. Determining the optimum size is not an easy task. Cole et al, (1998) for example, indicated that a special school should not fall below the mid-fifties if the entitlement to a broad and balanced curriculum was to be met. They also indicate that this should not be taken prescriptively because so many other factors need to be taken into account.

Wilson and Evans (1980) and Cole et al (1998) found that children with EBD appreciate environments characterised by regular patterns to the day, stability and good order. Redl (1966) talked of the 'great ego-supportive power of traditionalised routine'. Pupils with EBD feel more secure when in the company of staff who are able to create an orderly environment, who display firmness, fairness and yet a responsiveness to individual need. However, a balance has to be achieved between structure and a rigid, coercive environment. In latter circumstances, teachers tend to blame the children for their lack of success (Peagram, 1995), yet more recent research (Farrell, 1995) locates the source of the problem not within the child but within the school. Cole et al (1998) indicate that what is required is a 'rubber boundary' i.e. a structure and set of routines which provide support but are capable of movement to accommodate individual needs.

Effective interventions would appear to occur in institutions which are 'open' (Thomas, Walker and Webb, 1998; Daniels et al, 1999). They are open in the sense that all members of the institution and members of the surrounding community are able to access the systems and processes of the institution. Part of that openness is the ability to communicate and collaborate well, both internally within the school and externally with the community outside.

Effective intervention requires institutions to actively work with other agencies to meet the ecosystemic needs of pupils. Whilst this has been argued over for many years (Wilson and Evans, 1980, are an early example but see also Cole et al, 1998) it is only in recent times that moves have been made to provide a national lead in multi-agency approaches (DfEE, 1998). Many schools have pioneered work with a range of agencies. However, the evidence suggests (Cole at al, 1998) that this has been achieved more on a 'personal-professional' level. This form of inter-agency work is dependent upon personal relationships. When professionals move on these arrangements fall by the wayside. There is little evidence of structured formalised systematic arrangements for inter-agency working.

Conclusion

This chapter has attempted to give an overview of some of the issues on institutional interventions. It does not pretend to be comprehensive. Rather it reflects some of the biases of the writer. Interventions for pupils with EBD will continue to grow and expand. What is required in the future is for the changes to be more evidence-based rather than reactive. Interventions need to be evaluated and scrutinised, particularly in terms of their long-term outcomes so that a body of evidence can emerge upon which decisions can be made to meet the needs of pupils with EBD.

References

Apter, S.J. (1982) *Troubled Children, Troubled Systems.* New York: Pergamon.

Ayers, H. Clarke, D. and Murray, A. (1995) *Perspectives on Behaviour: A Practical Guide to Effective Interventions for Teachers.* London: David Fulton.

Bronfenbrenner, U. (1979) *The Ecology of Human Development.* Cambridge MA: Harvard University Press.

Bull, K. (1995) On common ground. *Special Children* 83, pp18-20.

Chamberlin, C. and Chamberlin, L. (1993) Alternative schools as a critique of traditional schools: the TVIND schools in Denmark. *Canadian Social Studies* 27, 3, 115 - 120.

Circulars 8/94 & 9/94 (1994) Behaviour Difficulties and Pupils with Emotional and Behavioural Problems. In (DfE 1994) *Pupils with Problems Pack.* London: DfE.

Clarke, D. and Murray, A. (1996) *Developing and Implementing a Whole School Behaviour Policy: A Practical Approach.* London: David Fulton.

Cole, T. Visser, J. and Upton, G. (1998) *Effective Schooling for Pupils with Emotional and Behavioural Difficulties.* London: David Fulton.

Connor, M. (1994) 'Emotional and Behavioural Disorders: Classification and Provision.' *Therapeutic Care and Education* Vol. 3 No. 1.

Cooper, P. (1993) *Effective Schools for Disaffected Pupils.* London: Routledge.

Cooper , P. (1996) 'Pupils as partners: pupils' contributions to the governance of schools' in Jones, K. and Charlton, T. (Ed) *Overcoming Learning and Behaviour Difficulties - Partnership with Pupils.* London: Routledge.

Cooper, P. Smith, C. and Upton, G. (1994) *Emotional and Behavioural Difficulties: Theory into Practice.* London: Routledge.

Coulby, J. and Coulby, D. (1989) 'Intervening in junior classrooms' in Docking, J. (Ed) *Education and Alienation in the Junior School.* London: Falmer.

Daniels, H., Hey, V., Leonard, D., and Smith, M. (1996) *Gender and Special Needs Provision in Mainstream Schooling.* London: ESRC.

Daniels, H., Visser, J., Cole, T. with de Reybekill, N. (1998) *Emotional and Behavioural Difficulties in Mainstream Schools Research Report RR90.* London: DfEE.

DES (1978) *Report of the Committee of Enquiry into the Education of Handicapped Children and Young People.* The Warnock Report. London: HMSO.

DES (1989a) *Discipline in Schools* (The Elton Report). London: HMSO.

DES (1989b) *A Survey of Pupils with Emotional/Behavioural Difficulties in Maintained Special Schools and Units. Report by HMI.* London: HMSO.

DfE (1994) *Code of Practice on the Identification and Assessment of Special Educational Needs.* London: HMSO.

DfEE (1997) *Excellence for All Children.* London: HMSO.

DfEE (1998) *A Programme for Action.* London: The Stationery Office.

DfEE (1999) *Social Inclusion: Pupil Support Circular 10/99.* London: DfEE.

Farrell, P. (1995) 'Emotional and behavioural difficulties: causes, definition and assessment' in Farrell, P. (Ed) *Children with Emotional and Behavioural Difficulties - Strategies for Assessment and Intervention.* London: Falmer Press.

Fullan, M. (1993) *Change Forces - Probing the Depths of Educational Reform.* London: Falmer Press.

Galloway, D. (1990) *Pupil Welfare and Counselling.* London: Longman.

Galloway, D. and Goodwin, C. (1987) *The Education of Disturbing Pupils.* London: Longman.

Garbarino, J. (1980) 'Some thoughts on school size and its effects on adolescent development.' *Journal of Youth and Adolescence* 9, 1, pp19-31.

Garner, P. and Gains, C. (1996) 'Models of intervention for children with emotional and behavioural difficulties.' *Support for Learning* 11, 4, pp141-145.

Greenhalgh, P. (1994) *Emotional Growth and Learning.* London: Routledge.

Grimshaw, R. with Berridge, D. (1994) *Educating Disruptive Children; Placement and Progress in Residential Special Schools for Pupils with EBD.* London: National Children's Bureau.

Gustavsen, B. (1996) 'Action research, democratic dialogues and the issue of "critical mass" in change.' *Qualitative Enquiry* 2, 1, pp90-103.

Jenkinson, J. (1997) *Mainstream or Special? Educating Students with Disabilities.* London: Routledge.

Kounin, J. (1970) *Discipline and Group Management in Classrooms.* New York: Krieger.

Kyriacou, C. (1991) *Essential Teaching Skills.* Hemel Hempstead: Simon and Schuster.

Laslett, R. (1977) *The Education of Maladjusted Pupils.* London: Granada.

Laslett R. (1995) 'Beliefs and Practice in the Early Schools for Maladjusted Children.' *Maladjustment and Therapeutic Education* Vol.1 No 4.

Laslett, R. Cooper, P. Maras, P. Rimmer, P. and Law, B. (1998) *Changing Perceptions: Emotional and Behavioural Difficulties Since 1945.* Maidstone: AWCEBD.

Long, R. (1999) Interventions for Inclusion, Unit 3 for EDSE 07 Distance Education course. School of Education, University of Birmingham.

Lund R. (1990) 'Curriculum Development for Children with EBD and the Introduction of the National Curriculum.' *Maladjustment and Therapeutic Education*, Vol. 8 No 1. East Sutton: AWCEBD.

McGilchrist, B. Mortimore, P. Savage, J. and Beresford, C. (1995) *Planning Matters.* London: Paul Chapman.

Meighan, R. and Toogood, R. (1992) *Anatomy of Choice in Education.* Ticknall: Education Now.

Ministry of Education (1955) *Report of the Committee on Maladjusted Children.* The Underwood Report. London: HMSO.

Molnar, A. and Lindquist B. (1989) *Changing Problem Behaviour in Schools.* San Francisco: Jossey-Bass.

Montgomery, D. (1989) *Managing Behaviour Problems.* London: Hodder and Stoughton.

Nanton, P. (1995) 'Extending the Boundaries: equal opportunities as social regulation.' *Policy and Politics* 23, 3, pp203-212.

OFSTED (1993) *Achieving Good Behaviour in Schools.* London: HMSO.

OFSTED (1995) *Framework for the Inspection of Special Schools.* London: HMSO.

Ogilvy, C.M. (1994) 'An evaluation review of approaches to behaviour problems in the secondary school.' *Educational Psychology* 14, 2, pp195-206.

Orr, R. (1995) 'A prescription for failure.' *Special Children* September, pp24-25.

Peagram, E. (1995) 'The foolish man built his house upon the sand.' *Therapeutic Care and Education* 4, 1, pp9-16.

Redl, F. (1966) *When We Deal With Children.* New York: Free Press.

Reid, K. (1987) 'The Hargreaves report, school improvement and absenteeism' in Reid, K. (Ed.) *Combating School Absenteeism.* London: Hodder and Stoughton.

Reinert, H. and Huang, A. (1987) *Children in Conflict.* New York: Merrill.

Riding, R. and Rayner, S. (1998) *Cognitive Styles and Learning Strategies: Understanding Style Differences in Learning and Behaviour.* London: David Fulton.

Rutter, M., Maughan, B., Mortimore, P. and Ouston, J. (1979) *Fifteen Thousand Hours, Secondary Schools and their Effects on Children.* Shepton Mallet: Basic Books.

Smith, C. and Laslett, R. (1993) *Effective Classroom Management.* London: Routledge.

Stoll, L. and Fink, D. (1994) 'School effectiveness and school improvement: some voices from the field.' *School Effectiveness and School Improvement* 5, 2, pp144-177.

Stone, L. (1990) *Managing Difficult Children in School.* Oxford: Blackwell.

Tattum, D. (1989) 'Alternative approaches to disruptive behaviour' in Jones, N. (Ed) *School Management and Pupil Behaviour.* Lewes: Falmer Press.

Thomas, G., Walker, D. and Webb, J. (1998) *The Making of the Inclusive School.* London: Routledge.

Topping K. (1983) *Educational Systems for Disruptive Adolescents.* London: Croom Helm.

Topping, K. (1990 'Disruptive pupils: changes in perception and provision' in Scherer, M., Gersch, I. and Fry, L. (Ed) *Meeting Disruptive Behaviour: Assessment, Intervention and Partnership.* London: Macmillan.

Visser J. (1993) *Differentiation: Making It Work.* Tamworth: NASEN.

Visser, J. and Cole, T. (1996) 'An overview of English special school provision for children with emotional and behavioural difficulties.' *Emotional and Behavioural Difficulties* 1, 3, pp11-16.

Wheldall, K. and Merrett, F. (1992) 'Effective classroom management' in Wheldall, K. (Ed) *Discipline in Schools: Psychological Perspectives on the Elton Report.* London: Routledge.

Wilson and Evans (1980) *Education of Disturbed Children.* London: Methuen.

Yarworth, J.S. and Gauthier, W.J. (1978) 'Relationship of student self concept and selected personal variables to participation in school activities.' *Journal of Educational Psychology* 70, pp335-344.

Chapter Eight

Managing Aggression and Responding to Violence

by Bernard Allen

Staff working with young people who have a history of emotional and behavioural difficulties should anticipate that they may be faced with aggression and sometimes violence. The best indicator of future behaviour is past behaviour, so it is reasonable to assume that young people who have behaved aggressively before are likely to do so again. It would be naïve of staff to hope that difficult situations will not arise, and negligent of managers to omit training in how to respond to violence effectively and safely.

The whole issue of how we should best deal with anger and aggression is complicated and controversial. In the years following the introduction of the *Children Act 1989* strong passions were aroused over how aggressive and violent children and young people should be managed. This period also saw a corresponding increase in the numbers of professional staff who found themselves suspended. Many of these cases followed accusations that staff had behaved inappropriately in the way they dealt with incidents of violence and aggression involving children and young people. Sometimes legal issues were clouded by confusion over non-statutory guidance and also philosophical considerations. This chapter looks at these issues by firstly considering the nature of aggression and violence within the educational context, and then considering the question of a professional response.

The nature of aggression and violence

The implications of aggression and violence are by their nature social, yet have a profound effect upon the individual themselves, and perhaps not surprisingly, impact upon the educational context. Defining violent behaviour or aggressive tendency is only the beginning of an attempt to come to terms with this topic. More important, perhaps, is the effect of such behaviour, both for the person and those around them. For these reasons, the nature of aggression and violence is treated in this discussion as a problem. Recognising and dealing with this problem is viewed as a first concern for the individual themselves as well as those supporting that individual, as they attempt to reach an understanding of the behaviour.

(1) Catharsis - 'getting it out of your system'

The philosophical arguments surrounding the area of aggression and violence go to the heart of our beliefs about how we can best help children and young people with emotional and behavioural difficulties. A strong element in the therapeutic tradition, which for many years was the dominant influence in this work, was the concept of catharsis. This is the idea that aggression builds up like pressure in a hydraulic system and venting anger releases that pressure. This is certainly a good metaphor for describing the way anger feels, and it was used first in ancient Greece. An important question, however, remains whether catharsis actually works – does it help to let people 'get it out of their system'?

The fact that Freud revived the idea and based much of his work upon it added respectability to the theory. Part of the therapeutic tradition maintains that 'acting out' is an essential part of the process of coming to terms with repressed anger. According to this hypothesis encouraging people to express aggression in a safe environment can be beneficial, and 'venting' the anger will reduce the risk of violent behaviour. Such ideas have resulted in angry people being advised to punch a pillow or a punch bag. People are sometimes encouraged to imagine the inanimate object is the person with whom they are angry and punching. These notions permeate popular psychology and the media to such an extent that many people believe there must be research evidence to support them.

In fact research evidence does not support the catharsis theory. It may feel good to beat up a cushion, but things that feel good are not necessarily beneficial. Bushman, Baumeister and Stack (1999) described the theory's record in research as 'dismal'. They confirm previous findings that performing cathartic activities fails to reduce subsequent aggression and violence, but in fact it increases it. The time has come to challenge the widely held belief that encouraging people to express their anger helps them manage their aggression, when in fact the opposite is the case. Some people gradually wind themselves towards violence. If there is no benefit in allowing people to become angry we should endeavour to take action early on to divert escalating confrontations and help people to develop and maintain self-control. Following this argument there may be circumstances in which it would be more sensible to take early action to prevent a slowly escalating confrontation, rather than waiting until damage has already occurred. Staff should anticipate what is likely to happen and take positive action to prevent the risk of harm increasing.

(2) Learning Aggression and Violence

People who are prone to aggression and violence are also often interested in violent games and videos. Once again the view that indulging in imagined aggression or violence can reduce the risk of real violence is not supported by research evidence. Therefore it follows that staff are justified in encouraging children and young people with emotional problems away from play-fighting and violent games.

Just as fantasy, fiction and games can stimulate aggressive feelings, they can also stimulate other feelings. Many people have experienced the dramatic effect an uplifting film, or good book, can have in bringing about a mood change. Sad stories can reduce people to tears, and so can happy ones leave a positive sense of well-being. These are examples of induced mood change. The effect can be sustained so that once you have induced a mood it influences people's whole perception of their world. Staff can influence the emotional climate by taking care over what forms of activity and entertainment are available.

(3) Dealing with Angry Feelings

People who are prone to aggression can learn to recognise the tell-tale signs when they are getting angry, and identify the sort of things that set them off. If they can recognise the signs, and remember to remove themselves from the situation, practise relaxation techniques and habitually think about the problem in a different way, they can learn to better manage their own behaviour.

When some people get angry they learn to make themselves angrier. Some people habitually talk to themselves in such a way that they spur themselves on towards violence. They keep dwelling on what another person has done to them, or how unfairly other people treat them, and rehearsing what they would like to do to get even and they get more and more angry, and more and more dangerous.

It can be helpful for people who are prone to episodes of escalating aggression and violence to learn to recognise the unhelpful things they say to themselves, and learn more effective ways of thinking. This 'self-instructional' training was developed from the work of Russian psychologists Vygotsky (1962) and Luria (1961), who identified that children control their own behaviour by talking to themselves, but as they get older this becomes internalised. Helping people to develop different thinking habits is sometimes called 'cognitive behavioural' therapy.

At another level, non-competitive physical exercise disperses the body chemicals that build up when people are frustrated, so providing opportunities to exercise may reduce the risk of aggression. Relaxing music has been shown to relax people, and certain colour schemes may be more relaxing than others. It is worth looking at all the aspects of the environment that are under our control. People can be taught relaxation techniques focusing on breathing control.

(4) Solution-Focused Brief Therapy

An alternative approach aimed at supporting the individual in improving self-management and thereby dealing with aggression and feelings of anger, is to consider the relevance of counselling. Models or theories of counselling may offer ways of achieving change by using counselling skills or strategies within the school context (as distinguished from psychotherapy associated with clinical interventions). One such approach, which has been gaining converts over recent years, is solution-focused brief therapy.

This practical, pragmatic form of counselling begins from the assumption that problems result from ineffective interaction patterns. It is also based on the belief that a small change in any part of the system can have a significant ripple effect. So there is not necessarily a need for huge, expensive, time-consuming meetings to enable solutions to be found. Two major guidelines of solution-focused therapy are 'if it works do more of it', and 'if it doesn't work do something different' (De Shazer, 1991).

Often, in schools, staff find it difficult to do something different, even when the strategies they have adopted are not working. People tend to respond by applying the same strategies more vigorously. An alternative is to look for exceptions to the problem, trying to identify what is different when the problem does not occur, or occurs less frequently. Murphy (1994) suggested that it is sometimes more effective to increase existing successes rather than eliminate problems directly.

(5) Promoting a Positive Atmosphere

Finally, understanding and working with the problem of aggression and violence will always be closely related to a 'social climate' or milieu. Schools, like other groups, organisations and communities are characterised by a number of traits which form a particular ethos. One such characteristic is aggression, and sometimes violence, which is found within that community. An organisational climate or ethos plays an important part in influencing the extent and form aggression and violence take within the community. This fact underlines the importance of school staff staying aware of the effect of the ethos, of ways in which they contribute to that same ethos, and also opportunities for deliberately using whole-school approaches to further influence the good management of aggression and violence.

One simple way to promote a more positive atmosphere is for staff to deliberately and calculatedly increase the ratio of positive to negative comments they make. This does not come naturally and requires practice, but the benefits are significant (Cole, Visser & Upton, 1998, p122).

Some schools can become caught up in a negative spiral of direction and punishment in which conflict and aggression feature heavily. It is in everyone's interests to ensure that sanctions are kept to the minimum that achieves the objective, and to build upon successes however small they may be.

Professional responses to violent or aggressive behaviour
There are several levels of response that typically structure a school's approach to aggression and violence. The first is a personal response and the management of conflict exercised by individual members of staff. The second is the shared approach adopted by a school staff which incorporates planned systems of school discipline and codes of conduct. A third and more general response involves an institutional approach to violence reflected in the formal management of aggression, philosophical values articulated by school leaders and its established ethos. The latter may be indicated in various ways, for example, use of permanent exclusion or use of sanctions and punishment.

(1) Personal Responses and Conflict Management
For the individual teacher in the school context, there are a number of basic points to consider when thinking through the question of a personal response to aggression, violent behaviour or conflict management. These include remaining alert to several aspects of interpersonal behaviour including non-verbal behaviour, posture, body language, self-awareness. *Non-verbal behaviour*: there is a considerable body of research evidence which shows that we underestimate the importance of non-verbal communication in social interactions (Argyle, 1988). In a crowded room or in a lift, people feel anxious because they are too close for comfort. They try to compensate by increasing psychological distance, avoiding

eye contact and staring at the ceiling. Young people who are in a heightened state of anxiety may need more personal space than usual. They signal this by looking away, in the same way as we do in lifts, but staff sometimes misread the signs. It is by no means uncommon to hear teachers saying, 'Look at me when I am talking to you!' Some pupils with emotional and behavioural difficulties may also have a distorted perception of appropriate personal space, either misjudging by standing too close for comfort or feeling threatened at what is generally considered 'normal' social distance. We need to be particularly sensitive to proximity and give additional space when a pupil is becoming agitated.

Posture: sometimes adults inadvertently adopt a threatening stance. Standing face to face, or towering above a child, can be perceived as threatening. Seating arrangements, such as chairs of different heights, can also convey an unwanted message. To appear less threatening staff can stand or sit slightly at an angle. Adults can squat down to communicate at a similar level to a child. Sitting down, when a young person is becoming agitated, sends a clear signal that you do not want to escalate a confrontation.

Body language: staff do not have a choice about whether or not they communicate through body language. The only choice is over whether or not they manage the signals they send. Staff need to be aware of the body language they project. Body language is particularly important when staff are trying to calm a distressed or angry young person. They should try to keep still and avoid waving arms around and gesticulating. They should try to use open palmed gestures, stand at a distance and at an angle, and avoid aggressive gestures such as clenched fists or pointing fingers. These can provoke a violent response. Prolonged eye contact is also threatening, but avoiding eye contact can signal fear, indecision, lack of confidence or lack of interest. The body language we wish to project is calm, assertive, caring and confident.

Self-awareness: staff need to be particularly aware of their own emotional responses, and be alert to the warning signs. When people are angry or frightened a number of physiological changes take place which gradually impair our ability to act effectively. The blood supply is diverted away from the small muscle groups, so that we are becoming less technically proficient, and from the brain so we become less able to make good balanced judgements.

Anyone who has been involved in a serious incident which has lasted for more than a couple of minutes is very likely to be subject to these changes. That is another reason why new people need to be involved wherever possible.

(2) Shared Responses and Conflict Management

For the professional staff in the school context, there are a number of basic points to consider when thinking through the question of a school-based response to aggression, violent behaviour or conflict management. These include sharing principles underpinning teamwork, establishing a shared script or protocol for handling violent or aggressive incidents at work and building safe systems of work.

Teamwork: in any escalating incident it is a good idea to try to involve somebody not directly involved in the incident, as frequently as possible. Each time an angry person focuses their anger on whoever they are faced with, a change of personnel can provide an opportunity for the confrontation to change direction. This is particularly true during physical restraint. It can be a good policy to agree that in any restraint situation colleagues will offer to take over, and that the offer will always be accepted. This is one way of preventing situations from becoming personal.

Recovery and following through: the period immediately after an episode of physical restraint can be particularly dangerous for staff. The internal body chemistry takes time to subside, even when the young person seems calm. During this recovery period, as staff try to rebuild relationships, the young person is particularly fragile and can be provoked to extreme violence very quickly and very easily. It is not uncommon for the young person to be depressed following a violent incident. It is crucial that staff are vigilant to that possibility. This is not yet the time for a post-mortem on all the errors of judgement which may have contributed to the incident. It is better to reserve this time for calming reassurance, and revisit the issues later when things are calmer. However, in busy workplaces this may not happen spontaneously unless robust systems are in place to ensure these matters are followed through.

Building safe systems of work: safe systems of work consist of risk assessments to identify and hopefully eliminate some of the factors that contribute to aggression and violence. Risk assessments can look at fixtures and fittings, aspects of the building, the structuring of the day and staff deployment. We learn from our experiences when we are genuinely interested in finding out where and when problems are occurring, what happens in the lead-up and what tends to happen afterwards. Good systems of reporting, recording, monitoring and review enable patterns to be discerned which might otherwise be missed. They also enable policies and guidelines to be continually developed and improved. But if recording and reporting systems are going to function they should be simple and easy to use. This is particularly true because the people who have to use these forms may not be performing at their best. People under pressure find it difficult to focus on the key issues that need to be recorded. Tick-lists can reduce the pressure, and structured forms help to guide the member of staff through the incident identifying all the salient points.

(3) Institutional Responses and Conflict Management

Managers and leaders in school have an administrative responsibility to ensure provision is made for health and safety in the workplace environment. Equally, they have an educational responsibility to ensure the well-being and personal development of every member of the school community. The latter involves the articulation of key attitudes and values as well as taking a lead in establishing and maintaining a school ethos. Generally, it is important that senior managers actively seek to support staff in their attempts to effectively manage aggression and violent behaviour. Similarly, support and guidance should be available which helps staff meet their responsibility to carry out their duty of care.

Promoting Health and Safety: Moore and Norman (1997), suggest that a constructive way of addressing the issue of conflict management in the workplace is to use a Health and Safety approach. The authors point out that failing to provide adequate training for staff could prove expensive for employers. Northumberland County Council paid £175,000 in compensation to a social worker in 1994 for failing to protect him from unreasonable stress. Failure to support and train staff who are vulnerable to personal abuse, threatening behaviour and physical attack could result in similar claims.

The Health and Safety regulations concerning the reporting of serious incidents, RIDDOR (Health and Safety Executive, 1995), included physical violence for the first time. Organisations involved in the care of people with emotional and behavioural difficulties should be encouraged to treat their training, policies and procedures as a Health and Safety issue. Using this approach managers should identify the nature and extent of any risk, devise measures to provide a safer workplace and devise measures to provide safer systems of work, as far as is reasonably practicable. It is not possible to guarantee absolute safety in care environments any more than it is on ships and in coal mines. The term 'reasonably practicable' means that employers will have to show that they have considered the issues and made a reasonable attempt to do something about it. Staff also have a duty to take reasonable steps to protect themselves and their colleagues. However, the overriding consideration in all our dealings with children is the welfare of the child.

Guidance and training: in its 1990 report, the Health and Safety Advisory Committee suggested that training for school staff should include: legal considerations, causes of violence and aggression, communication/ interpersonal skills, techniques for preventing and avoiding violence, calming aggressive people, advice on when physical restraint is appropriate, acceptable methods of restraint and techniques for breaking away from a violent person.

After almost ten years very few organisations could claim to have delivered such a comprehensive programme of training. An additional problem has been a lack of clear and consistent guidance from central Government and local authorities. Guidance has been much clearer about what staff may not do, rather than offering constructive advice about what they should attempt. In these circumstances there is always the risk that staff will find it easier to do nothing, rather than do the wrong thing.

There has also been a reluctance for the Government to acknowledge that what has been presented as clarification of previous advice was actually a change in policy in certain key areas. This may have reduced the impact of the revisions and slowed the dissemination of revised guidance in some local authorities.

Support for staff: in our attempts to promote a culture in which both employers and employees take responsibility for developing safe systems of work we should move away from what, for staff, has sometimes felt like a 'blame' culture. Wishful thinking by senior management can promote a view that violent incidents result in some way from failures on the part of the staff to de-escalate the situation. Some teams of management have tried to introduce policies forbidding all physical interventions, arguing that they did not need to train staff in anything other than interpersonal skills. The reality is that nobody, no matter how skilled or how well trained, can guarantee that interpersonal skills alone can successfully defuse every situation.

The quality of interpersonal skills is crucially important, and it is right to focus training on this area. But it is wrong to rely on it exclusively and neglect training in escape, and safe, effective physical restraint. A de-escalation strategy which works 90% of the time is a very good strategy indeed. But that means it will fail once in every ten incidents, even if staff do everything right. Staff need other strategies to fall back on. It is not an option to advise staff to avoid physical intervention at all costs, because some people have a duty of care which obliges them to act in the interests of the young people they are looking after. Following the introduction of the *Children Act 1989* several local authorities issued guidance which was interpreted as prohibiting physical restraint, citing the authority of the Act. More recent 'clarification' from both the DfEE and the DoH should correct some of the misapprehensions.

Duty of care: staff who are looking after children and young people have a duty of care which means that they are expected to act as a reasonable parent. One important aspect of parenting is to support and encourage children to try new things. Sometimes this involves gently pushing children when they lack confidence, for example learning to swim or ride a bike. But equally important is that aspect of parenting which involves holding children back, preventing them from taking ill-judged risks. We try to prevent toddlers from climbing stairs, we try to prevent young children from riding their bikes on the road, or from staying out late at night. In an ideal world, where all children had been brought up to be reasonable and co-operative, there would be no problem. But issues such as these can provoke conflict in children and young people who have emotional and behavioural difficulties. For staff who have a duty of care, to adopt avoidance strategies is an abrogation of their responsibilities.

Summary
Recent guidance from the Department of Health and the Department for Education and Employment reasserts the need for staff to act as reasonable parents, and to make an effort to control the youngsters in their care. Young people with emotional and behavioural difficulties may

exhibit aggression and violence. Organisations need to plan ahead using a Health and Safety model to assess and reduce risk. Staff need to be trained to calm escalating problems and manage violence safely and effectively. Children and young people need to be encouraged to take responsibility for controlling their own behaviour and helped to develop successful habitual patterns of interaction. Ignoring the issue will not make it go away. The more openly we can discuss the issues and develop better practice, the better prepared staff will be, and the safer the workplace will be for both them and the young people in their care.

References

Allen, B. (1998a) *Holding Back.* Bristol: Lucky Duck Publishing.

Allen, B. (1998b) 'New Guidance on the use of reasonable force in schools.' *British Journal of Special Education,* 25 (4), pp184-188.

Argyle, M. (1988) *Bodily Communication (2nd Edition).* London: Methuen.

Bushman, B. J., Baumeister, R. F. and Stack, A. (1999) 'Catharsis, Aggression, and Persuasive Influence Self-Fulfilling or Self-Defeating Prophecies?' *Journal of Personality and Social Psychology,* 76, (3), 367-376.

Cole, T., Visser J. and Upton G. (1998) *Effective Schooling for Pupils with Emotional and Behavioural Difficulties.* London: David Fulton Publishers.

Davies, W. and Frude, N. (1993) *Preventing Face to Face Violence: Dealing with Anger and Aggression at Work.* London: APT.

Department for Education and Employment (1998) *Circular 10/98: Section 550A of the Education Act 1996: The Use of Force to Control or Restrain Pupils.* London: DfEE.

De Shazer, S. (1991) *Putting difference to work.* New York: W. W. Norton.

Feindler E. L. and Ecton, R. B. (1986) *Adolescent Anger Control: Cognitive Behavioural Techniques.* Oxford: Pergamon.

Green, R. G. and Quanty, M. B. (1977) 'The catharsis of aggression: An evaluation of a hypothesis.' In L. Berkowitz (Ed), *Advances in Experimental Social Psychology (Vol 10, pp 1-37).* New York: Academic Press.

Health and Safety Advisory Committee (1990) *Violence to Staff in the Education Sector.* London: Health & Safety Advisory Committee.

Health and Safety Executive. (1995) *RIDDOR, Everyone's Guide to RIDDOR 95.* HSE Books, PO Box 1999, Sudbury, Suffolk CO10 6FS.

Laming, H. (1997) *The Control of Children in the Public Care: Interpretation of the Children Act 1989.* London: Department of Health.

Luria, A. (1961) *The Role of Speech in the Regulation of Normal and Abnormal Behaviours.* New York: Liveright.

Lyon, C. (1994) *Legal Issues Arising from the Care, Control and Safety of Children with Learning Disabilities who also present challenging behaviour.* London: The Mental Health Foundation.

Moore, W. and Norman, G. (1997) *Responding to Violence: A model for Health and Care Agencies.* London: Prepare Publications.

Murphy, J. J. (1994) 'Working with what works: Solution-focused approach to school behaviour problems.' *The School Counsellor*, 42, 59-65.

Spence. S. (1995) *Social Skills Training: Enhancing Social Competence with Children and Adolescents.* London: NFER-Nelson

Vygotsky, L. (1962) *Thought and Language.* New York: Wiley.

Chapter Nine

The Prevention of EBD: Frameworking inter-agency involvement

by Dave Shaw

> 'I said to her: "If you have four really good days at school
> and one bad one, what do people remember?"
> She replied: "the bad one".'
>
> (Fletcher-Campbell, 1997:78)

Looked-after young people are surrounded by a myriad of support workers and welfare services professionals. Intervening in the life of any one youngster who is looked after may be LEA officers, educational psychologists, child psychiatrists, special educational needs support staff, educational welfare officers, therapists, field and residential social workers, review managers, foster carers and youth justice workers - all of these in addition to the usual set of professionals with whom any child will have contact such as teachers, general practitioners and the health visitor. Their families may well be involved in aspects of life associated with poverty and stress, debt and rent arrears, the police and unemployment. Some will be embroiled within the personal chaos and litigation of violence and abuse.

Although many will survive such circumstance and trauma and lead relatively normal lives, many will exhibit and bring with them into school all the 'baggage and symptoms' associated with youngsters defined as having 'emotional and behavioural difficulties'. They will inevitably present to schools a serious challenge in successfully meeting their educational needs. In some cases this challenge goes beyond the realms of what individual schools can manage and poses questions as to how society at large can meet the educational rights of youngsters who, through circumstance and their behaviour, may stretch to the absolute limits what society can provide.

The practice for professionals working with young people who are looked after is typically organised on an individual basis and called case-load. Given the potential for so many professionals to be involved with looked-after youngsters, there is a danger that the slightest misconception of intent or unclear perception of role or understanding in the development and progress of a case can and will have the potential to compound the problems with which the family are already confronted. The result of this will be further disruption to lives already characterised by insecurity, instability and fragmentation.

This chapter is concerned with the interface between social services and schools in relation to children who are looked-after. Throughout the discussion 'social services' will refer to the carers, social workers, foster carers and others associated with social service departments for all looked-after children in their care. 'Schools' will refer to all that a local education authority can provide in terms of the education of looked-after children but will primarily be concerned with the actions of teachers in meeting their educational needs. The issues to be raised include discussion of the perceptions held in both camps about the other, together with a suggestion as to how the two sides might come together in a possible framework of joint working. This approach is aimed at helping to ensure that each looked-after youngster has full access to all that schools can provide and is therefore enabled to grasp this opportunity in order to reach their full potential. The parallels along the way in relation to the general understanding and management of pupils defined as exhibiting 'emotional and behavioural difficulties' will be apparent to the reader.

Educational provision for children looked after by the Local Authority

The evidence is compelling that looked-after youngsters get a raw deal when they go to school. The *Times Educational Supplement* of March 5th 1999 had the headline 'Children in care failed by councils', a conclusion arrived at by a survey which revealed that 39% of local authorities in England have no information about what their children in care achieved in school at 16. Furthermore, two-thirds of the LEAs surveyed did not know how their looked-after children did in national tests (Gold, 1999).

Figures taken from the House of Commons select committee second report on Children Looked-After by Local Authorities, published in July 1998, were analysed by Slater and Palmer (1999). They found that:

- 26% of looked-after 14 to 16 year-olds were receiving no education.
- Around 75% of care-leavers have no qualifications at all compared with 6% of all other 16 year-olds.
- Fewer than 20% of care-leavers stay on post-16, compared to 68% of all 16 year-olds.

Such statistics highlight and reflect how youngsters who come into the care system in whatever way and for whatever reason, may not be in a position to make appropriate responses to normal situations and hence fail to capitalise on the opportunities school has to offer. This is a significant issue for practice, given the rhetoric that such youngsters might best be served within schools by being treated just the same as everyone else. 'Discrete support' in this sense, with the excuse that to single out a child 'in-care' will provoke and carry with it the dangers and burdens of labelling and stigma, can become so intangible as to be invisible and hence lost.

The notion that looked-after youngsters can be left to sink or swim in amongst the rest of their peers is no longer acceptable. Positive intervention is vital and necessary not just for the personal benefit of each youngster but also for the amelioration of its social impact on a wider scale. For example, 38% of all young offenders and 30% of all homeless people have been in care. Again, 50% of all leavers who 'are in-care' are unemployed (see the House of Commons select committee 2nd report on Children Looked-After by Local Authorities, published in July 1999, quoted from the *Times Educational Supplement*, 5/3/99).

The above statistics reveal the current extent of the problem. However, more detailed research into the education of children in care in the past has been lacking. It is only comparatively recently that the issue of the poor performance of children in care has become a concern. The NFER were among the first to address this concern. They capitalised on work undertaken by Sonia Jackson (1987), who highlighted the fact that little work had been done in this area. The resultant NFER Report (Fletcher-Campbell & Hall, 1990) was able to identify some of the problems and point to what might need to be done to address these but did not, at that time, find evidence from local authorities of any coherent or structured good practice on which to base further research.

Both the Utting Report (1991) and the Warner Report (1992) identified and stressed the importance of the role of education for the children for whom social services were involved. The Audit Commission (1994), whilst investigating the co-ordination across community provision for children in need, stressed that the education of such children was problematic and noted that social services staff blamed education departments for not providing sufficient alternative education whilst education officers criticised social services staff for not intervening early enough with vulnerable families to prevent difficulties arising in school placements. The commissioners noted, somewhat succinctly, that *meanwhile children missed their education* (Audit Commission, 1994: paragraph 95, quoted in Fletcher-Campbell, 1997:3).

Similarly, a joint circular from the Department of Health and the Department of Education (DfEE, 1994) set out guidance for the role of schools and carers, stressing the importance of inter-agency collaboration aimed at ensuring that the education of looked-after children was effectively managed. The circular pulled no punches stating that, *wherever children looked-after are placed, their education should always be a prime consideration and the various authorities involved should always co-operate to see that effective educational provision is made* (Fletcher-Campbell, 1997: p20).

Another joint evaluation published by the Office of Standards in Education (OFSTED) and the Social Services Inspectorate (SSI) (1995) identified the poor performance of children looked-after in schools, pointing out to the low priority given to education by professionals working with them. There was also evidence of poor liaison and lack of co-ordination between services, inadequate communication and management of information, reported lethargy in decision making and a negligible amount of specific training for relevant professionals. A final recommendation stated was that:

> 'As a matter of urgency SSD, LEAs and schools need to work together to devise ways of ensuring an appropriate educational placement and entitlement for these children.'
> (OFSTED/SSI, 1995: p44, para 92).

To reach the turn of the millennium, and yet still have what appears to be such a gaping hole in the educational provision of a small yet significant element of the school population is, to put it mildly, concerning. The fact that the plight of the looked-after child, educationally, has been brought into focus by the above reports, is a major step forward. The 'problem' now that it has been accepted, however, is only a beginning. The next step is to ask the question, how are we going to effect a change?

Inter-agency working: joining up solutions

From the argument previously outlined, it is possible to point up a direction professionals might take in order to move things forward. The immediate challenge might be seen as being about translating rhetoric into the reality of positive action. What this will mean for traditionally held notions of the professional boundaries and expertise between social services and schools will form part of a movement towards better collaboration between various agencies working with young people. Questions arise fairly quickly and pointedly. How can changes be made which will not only drastically improve the educational chances of looked-after children but also not threaten the established order of professional roles and responsibilities? In the light of the statistical evidence, there is a clear mandate for change but how should this change be managed?

One traditional view which might prevent this kind of change occurring is the argument that generally, social services and schools have always worked together but in a separate fashion. Without wishing to totally throw out all past practice and acknowledging that there must have been some isolated pockets of good practice, however, it is glaringly obvious that all has not been well in regards to the education of young people in care. The differences in approach are perhaps reflected in one comment of a respondent in the NFER survey of working practice, who stated that *Social Services deals with 2% of the population and is very resource intensive; the LEA deals with 100% of the relevant population and resources are spread extensively* (Fletcher-Campbell, 1997:13). It is possible to accept that each profession has differing priorities and ways of conceiving of clients but looks towards working collaboratively in order to meet the needs of the individual!

In the NFER survey, for example, another respondent captured some of the difficulties experienced by workers in the field, who said, *Social Services are responsible for vulnerable kids who are usually messing things up for school* (Fletcher-Campbell, 1997:14). The clear expectation is that social workers are facing a difficult task in supporting the undesirable and the rejected. Finally, one interviewee summed up the challenge when they stated that *the key challenge is the interface between the two agencies and how we achieve it without wasting energy in terms of who controls the service* (Fletcher-Campbell, 1997:14). The rhetoric of 'joined-up solutions', which is after all a necessary aim, requires developing new approaches to case-work and SEN provision. These approaches need to enable professionals in different agencies to work collaboratively in and out of schools to support young people who are at risk of missing out on an education.

In a concerted effort to address what it sees as a general failure of our child care systems, the Government, in September 1998, launched *Quality Protects: A Framework for Action* (Dept. of Health, 1998). This described a three year programme aimed at improving local authority children's services in health, social services and education so that they are well managed, integrated, effective and accountable. Quality Protects mandates local authorities to set clear objectives, linked to a new children's services grant of £375 million and dependent on authorities meeting targets and performance indicators, which for the first time set out clear outcomes for children and in some instances give precise targets which local authorities are expected to achieve.

As part of the programme local authorities are encouraged to regard the educational attainment of their looked-after children as an indication of their general social well-being and sets sub-objectives which look to bring the overall performance of looked-after children in schools, at key stage SATs and GCSE, closer in line with their peers.

To bring about such progress the following targets were identified:

- July 2001   Target date for 50% plus of looked-after children to achieve one graded GCSE or equivalent by the age of 16
- July 2003   Target date for 75% plus of looked-after children to achieve one graded GCSE or equivalent at the age of 16.

Although perhaps a blunt instrument of change, the above targets at least set out to address the problem and mandate professionals to develop strategies to bring them about. A key element of the Quality Protects programme is the intention that all children's services should be fully integrated and work jointly to meet needs.

Although the rhetoric of 'working together' is generally accepted as a good thing to do, there have been problems, as shown by research carried out by Dyson, Lin and Millward (1998), which revealed a series of problems in securing and maintaining effective co-operation. These included delays and difficulties in the exchange of information between agencies with joint information handling systems virtually non-existent.

Schools found that it was difficult to identify appropriate contacts within Social Service Departments (SSDs) or to secure the kinds of interventions from SSDs which they thought appropriate.

Dyson et al (1998) reported that frequently there were 'border disputes' between departments over who was responsible for providing specific services, for example speech and language therapy. Sometimes interventions were made in the same case by two or more agencies with little or no dialogue between them. Parents reported that in some instances they felt that it was they who acted as co-ordinators between agencies. In general, problems in co-operation stemmed from the fact that different agencies work within differing legislative and organisational frameworks, operated with different definitions of need and pursued different priorities.

In contrast to the above, an area which has developed inter-agency working to an effective level, and therefore offers hope to both social services and schools, is the field of child protection. Hallett (1995) found that almost unanimously those interviewed accepted the importance of working together and appeared to value it, rejecting Blyth and Milner's (1990:195) observation that *given the opportunity, professionals would probably work better alone.*

Furthermore, as one social worker was reported by Hallett to have remarked:

> 'Sometimes inter-agency work, working with other agencies is difficult but I would prefer to work with other agencies. They've got expertise that I haven't got. They know, you know, and there's no getting away from that. If you come from a standpoint, which I do, that child protection is a multi-agency responsibility and it's a jigsaw and the social workers can't do it on their own, they need the other agencies to assist them, we haven't got all the skills right. We need other skill areas.'
>
> (Blyth and Milner, 1990: 297)

Perhaps the dilemma facing social services and schools at this stage of the development of joint working practices lies in the relative ignorance each has of the other side. It is possible to identify attitudes and prejudices which, although in some ways amusing, hold grains of truth which in reality should not be tolerated.

Frame-working collaborative support: integration, inclusion and progression

The notion of the '2CV driving do-gooding social worker' together with the 'stuffy, chalk dust covered teacher' (with the mandatory patches on each jacket elbow) does not really ring true. The joke turns sour when confronted by the evidence of the poor performance of looked-after youngsters in school and within the care system. Stereotypes become excuses and a rationale for apathy. Hallett (1995) commented that the development of effective joint working practices within child protection reflected such notions and referred to the evidence of professionals who, by having to work together, set up networks and mechanisms which enabled workers to see things from each other's point of view, to the benefit of their clients.

The interface between social services and schools is now at a stage, through the mandate of Quality Protects, where joint working practices will have to be developed and where systems and structures used in the past are subject to review. One way forward might be to adopt and expand suggestions of the kind put forward by Fletcher-Campbell (1997), who identified three concepts which need to be fully embraced by teachers and carers working with looked-after youngsters so that each might gain access to schooling in ways which will enable each youngster to be able to reach their full potential. The terms she used for these concepts are *integration, inclusion* and *progression*.

The terminology used has parallels in the world of special education where they are already well established and used more commonly. In many ways this is unfortunate. The labels we assign to working practices or approaches can have different levels of understanding and lead to differing expectations and outcomes depending on who is using them. Thinking that we 'know' what another professional is telling us and getting it wrong can cause tensions and weaken the confidence one worker will have of the other's ability to complete a task. Although not wishing to get into a tautological debate here, an explanation of the three concepts might best be understood in a context of how a looked-after youngster might be introduced to a new school situation where practitioners need to consider how best to bring the youngster into contact with the routines and culture of the school when, resulting out of the young person's past experiences, these may be alien and incomprehensible.

(1) Integration

For the successful integration of a looked-after youngster into this new situation, a partnership involving carers, teachers, and the young person, needs to be formed. The practicalities involved in establishing such a partnership, particularly when a young person has specific and often acute needs, is often beset with attention to detail that can easily be dismissed as trivial. Small things can so often result in a fall-out of massive proportion. This means that involved professionals need to pay attention, for example, to issues surrounding school uniform, bus timetables, dinner money, organising and being aware of which item of equipment is required for which day, be it PE equipment or the ingredients for the next home economics lesson. It will involve making visits to the school before the start date to introduce the youngster to significant members of staff and to familiarise them with the layout and atmosphere of the school. Teachers will need to ensure that all staff are aware of the impending newcomer and, without divulging sensitive information, will ensure that an appropriate induction programme will be carefully structured and monitored. Steps should also be taken to make sure that the class about to receive the newcomer is aware that an arrival is impending.

During the NFER study examining working practice, a carer stated that:

> 'If from the age of three, you have been accustomed, at mid-day, to awakening your parents, who are sleeping off the previous night's hangover, and to receiving a volley of abuse on so doing, this is 'normal' experience for you by your early teens. You cannot then be expected to make a sudden switch to fit in with the rest of the world without a transitional period. It is entirely unrealistic for adults to expect you to get up one morning, clean and dressed in school uniform, to arrive at school in time and do a full day's work. You need to start with a part-time afternoon programme and gradually be 'integrated' into the sort of routines that others follow and accept as normal. These new, and previously unknown routines and the culture which they represent, need also to be integrated into your lifestyle.'

(Fletcher-Campbell, 1997: 13)

A common complaint of social workers and carers, identified in the NFER study, was that some teachers assumed that all their pupils came from stable, middle class homes; they seemed to have no awareness of the intolerable traumas that some of their pupils were going through and the stresses that would tax an adult, let alone a child. Other social workers complained that some schools almost immediately took up a confrontational stance, demanding an explanation of why they should admit the looked-after youngster rather than consider strategies to facilitate the admission process.

For example, one social worker in the same study explained that they had approached X high school and

> '... they looked at the statement on the boy and said: "This kid's obviously got massive problems. Why should we take him on and why do you think he will be able to fit into mainstream school?" I went through the fact that he had gone through a term at primary school with no trouble and just had the support of a dinner lady who sat with him in the odd lesson to ensure he completed the set work.'
>
> (Fletcher-Campbell, 1997: 111)

The teacher continued to express a negative attitude, taking the view that the young person would not fit into the school. Integration was, in this example, an unlikely outcome.

(2) Inclusion

The NFER study found that it was the perceptions of adults, particularly teachers, which young people who were looked after by the local authority held, that represented a critical factor in the way in which they responded to their education. In this context, the term inclusion has a subtle meaning. It is concerned with how a youngster feels about the experience of being accepted and comfortable in school. Much of the ground work in terms of the practicalities of the integration process described above bears fruit at this stage of the induction process. By establishing a secure and structured context as previously described, the foundations are laid down. The development of trusting and positive relationships can then be built upon this foundation. There is double advantage to this approach, in the sense that not only will the youngster have a much better chance of establishing relationships with other pupils, but it will be apparent that the staff involved are working together. This, in turn, will also begin to foster the kinds of mutually supportive relationships which will help to ensure the success of the youngster's experience in school.

Crucial to the concept of inclusion is the acknowledgement and acceptance by both social services and schools that however problematic some aspects of the youngster's behaviour within the context of the classroom can be, it falls upon those involved in the task of meeting their needs to recognise that the behaviours exhibited have been arrived at through no fault of their own and should be seen as a process through which a youngster may well be communicating deep anxiety (Fletcher-Campbell, 1997: 11).

Achieving successful inclusion can be a difficult nut to crack given the obvious hurdles presented by the day-to-day routines, expectations and demands of life in school. A school, as Laslett observed,

> '... by its conventions, discipline and curriculum can continue and confirm children's alienating experiences. On the other hand, a school can support, stimulate and demonstrate care for those children already in difficulties, thus preventing or arresting their maladjustment.'
> (Laslett, 1982: 19).

The setting of boundaries and expectations in the classroom might best be developed within a positive framework as described by Greenhalgh (1994). The notion of 'emotional holding', as defined by Greenhalgh, was developed from the idea that an *... affirmative response to chaotic behaviours where the 'carer' essentially is attempting to boundary the 'boundaryless' individual in such a way as to achieve a meaningful space for both of them* (Adams, 1986). In this way, Greenhalgh argued, professionals were to be encouraged in conscious reflection upon the relationships and interventions they made with the children with whom they work.

It might be said that in this respect, teachers have a lot to learn from their social work colleagues, in that they have been primarily working with the 'sharp end' of the emotional development of their clients whilst teachers have been more concerned with their intellectual development. A crucial question here is how much should the teacher's role in school be devoted to the development of emotional support in an area more traditionally associated with that of the carer? If joint working under the mandate of Quality Protects is to facilitate emotional growth and learning, as described by Greenhalgh (1994), in ways which might encourage the blurring of the traditionally held notions of role boundaries, there is a danger that the teacher's primary task - to teach - might be deflected. The issues of role, role clarity and role overlap in the development of new joint working practices will need to be addressed if the targets set out in Quality Protects are to be attained.

The Tunbridge Report (DHSS, 1972) suggested that the lack of clear role definitions, inadequately defined responsibilities, inaccurate job descriptions, the overlap between complementary disciplines and the consequent significant duplication of effort could be a major cause of conflict. Coupe and Porter (1986) also specified the potential problems inherent in role uncertainty and role overlap. Hallett and Stevenson (1980) cited Robinson (1978, p203), who argued that *teachers, while paying attention to the world of the child outside the school situation, must focus on the educational tasks of the school.* The dilemma lies in the definition of what the educational tasks are and how teachers interpret their role.

The attitude of teachers, and the approach taken by schools will depend upon their philosophy and professional perspective. This will equally affect the way in which tasks are carried out within an inter-agency environment. At one extreme, according to Fitzherbert (1977:139), there may be headteachers who put forward the view *that the teacher's responsibility for his pupils ends at the school gates and at the end of the school day*, whilst at the other extreme, there will be headteachers who have *an overdosed sense of responsibility for the welfare of children* and who will *be of limited effectiveness unless it is coupled with the ability to share his load with others, outside professionals as well as fellow teachers* (p140).

An important question, therefore, is how far teachers ought to go in terms of a holistic approach to their work? Where should the line be drawn between the teacher's role and the welfare of pupils which might affect that role? Stanley (1994: 44) commented that *teaching is therapeutic but not therapy* and that *therapy cannot be teaching but can be educational*. In this sense, it is important for the carers and teachers to be clear about the complementary yet contrasting roles each has to play in the process. As Stanley (1994: 44) argued, there is a need to ... *assess the past history in the context of the here and now and to plan for a future using our task, role and function as that significant other in a child's life - as a teacher- keeping in mind the therapeutic without becoming a rival parent or therapist.* It is important that teachers and other agency professionals are clear about the tasks each are to perform within the context of the joint working practice, if at the very least not to confuse the youngster at the heart of the process. The chances for success, however, reflect the need for shared understanding and mutual support, in order that agreed goals are achieved.

(3) Progression

The third concept central to the education of looked-after children is that of 'progression' which can only be effectively measured through the degree of success and achievement the youngster will experience in school. In the data collected by the NFER study the concept of progression within the education system was 'noticeably lacking':

> 'All the research evidence about usual practice has, until recently, suggested that mere attendance at school, or containment within the system, has been the primary focus of most attention given to education.'
>
> (Fletcher-Campbell, 1997: 15)

Although it might be accepted that attendance at school over a sustained period will indeed be a very real achievement for a youngster more used to regular truancy, it must also be acknowledged that this only marks the restoration of the opportunity for that young person to begin to take advantage of the provision on offer.

Collaborative working still needs to be sustained and an awareness shared that within this attendance at school lies the opportunity to develop practice and strategies geared to the general and specific problems which the youngster might encounter along the way. In the NFER survey a social worker commented:

> '... I think I was aware that you can have a marvellous care package but if the education goes wrong, it is all hopeless... In the past, you felt the effect of educational failure, i.e. the care package collapsing, but didn't identify education as the critical element. I thought that education was something nice for them to do during the day - but not critical. Now social workers identify education as a crucial element in the whole package - to make other things work ... you're doomed to failure without it.'
>
> (Fletcher-Campbell, 1997: 13)

A useful strategy to employ which will help develop inter-agency working can be to combine social work and educational objectives. Inter-agency working in this context means more than each party just being aware of the other's situation. It should mean that each has an equal involvement in and influence over the day-to-day progress of the young person. Teachers should be involved in gathering evidence of success and achievement in the young person's learning and reporting back to carers. They, in turn, will keep teachers up to date on the relevant dynamics of the youngster's day-to-day home life.

A systematic recording of progress in school can provide tangible evidence of the youngster's accomplishments and progress. The latter will confirm and help to dispel any misunderstanding, apathy or conflict which might have once existed in the minds of those young people being supported in this way. The quotation taken from the NFER study, placed at the beginning of this chapter, reflects this argument. Youngsters used to viewing their experience of school in a negative light may be slow to respond to interventions until the penny drops that being in school is 'cool' and that they have at last got some investment in the process of education.

The discussion so far has outlined issues and processes which serve to build up a picture of joint working between social workers, carers and teachers. While this framework is perhaps not unique, it does at least put forward and develop a structure around which future development and progress can take place. Professional efforts in this respect must strive to redress the appalling status quo reflected in the statistics surrounding the current levels of performance of looked-after youngsters in schools.

The processes and strategies previously described, however, will only be truly effective if they are nurtured within an atmosphere of flexibility, competency and consistency. This, in turn, will usually lead to the development of trust and respect between all concerned. These final two conditions cannot be legislated for, or mandated by managers. They have to evolve from the processes of actually working together within a climate of successful intervention. Just as looked-after youngsters can be given a framework within which they can begin to make the most of their experience in school, so too can that same framework help the social worker, carer and teacher to develop their roles in ways which begin to challenge a wrong that has not been successfully addressed for far too long.

References

Adams, T. (1986) 'Holding and the Shadow - Holding On.' *Unpublished paper given at a conference organised by ILEA Schools Psychological Service,* London.

Audit Commission (1994) *Seen But Not Heard: Co-ordinating Community Child - Health and Social Services for Children in Need.* London: HMSO.

Blyth, E. and Milner, J. (1990) *The process of inter-agency work in Violence Against Children Study Group. Taking Child Abuse Seriously.* London: Unwin Hyman.

Coupe, J. and Porter, J. (1986) (Eds) *The Education of Children with Severe Learning Difficulties.* London: Croom Helm.

Department of Education and Employment and the Department of Health (1994) The Education of Children being Looked After by Local Authorities. *Circular Nos 13/94 and DH LAC (94).* London: DfEE.

Department of Health (1991) *Children in Public Care: A Review of Residential Care. The Utting Report.* London: HMSO.

Department of Health (1992) *Committee of Enquiry into the Selection, Development and Management of Staff in Children's Homes: The Warner Report 1992, Choosing with Care.* London: HMSO.

Department of Health: Social Services Inspectorate and Office for Standards in Education (1995) *The Education of Children Looked-After by Local Authorities.* London: HMSO.

Department of Health (1998) *Quality Protects: A Framework for Action.* London: HMSO.

Department of Health and Social Security (1972) *Rehabilitation: Report of a Sub- Committee of the Standing Medical Advisory Committee* (The Tunbridge Report). London: HMSO.

Dyson, D., Lin, M. and Millward, A. (1998) *Effective Communication between Schools, LEAs and the Health and Social Services in the field of Special Needs.* University of Newcastle on Tyne: Department of Education and Employment, Research Briefs, Report No. 60. Sudbury: DfEE Publications.

Fitzherbert, K. (1977) *Child Care Services and the Teacher.* London: Temple Smith.

Fletcher-Campbell, F. and Hall, C. (1990) *Changing Schools? Changing People? The Education of Children in Care.* Slough: NFER.

Fletcher-Campbell, F. (1997) *The Education of Children Who are Looked-After.* Slough: NFER.

Gold, K. (1999) 'Children in Care failed by Local Councils.' *The Times Educational Supplement,* 5th March 1999, p1, No. 4314.

Greenhalgh, P. (1994) *Emotional Growth and Learning.* London: Routledge.

Hallett, C. and Stevenson, O. (1980) *Child Abuse: Aspects of Inter-professional Co-operation.* London: Allen and Unwin.

Hallett, C. (1995) *Inter-Agency Co-ordination in Child Protection Studies in Child Protection.* London: HMSO.

Jackson, S. (1987) *The Education of Children in Care.* Bristol: University of Bristol, School of Applied Social Studies.

Laslett, R. (1982) *Maladjusted Children in the Ordinary School.* Stratford upon Avon: National Council for Special Education.

Slater, J. and Palmer, J. (1999) 'Analysis of the Children Looked-After by Local Authorities Report.' *The Times Educational Supplement,* 5th March 1999, pp22-24, No. 4314.

Stanley, J. (1994) *What is Therapy? What is Teaching?* East Sutton: AWCEBD, Charlton Court Publications.

The Times Educational Supplement (1999) *TES Leader, Opinion.* 5th March 1999, p16.

* QUOTE p 98

* P99 PRUs   Problem v solution focused.

p 100 Behav, psychod approach & ecosystemic

*R 101 eclectic app.

* 102 Whole sch behav pol. - pupil partic.

*R 103 4 principles of understanding behav. *

104 bring diff & disrupt behav.

104 Common traits in "   "

105 Class & lemon managent.

106 Positce relats itt pupils.